You Just Have to Laugh...

and I Can Prove It!

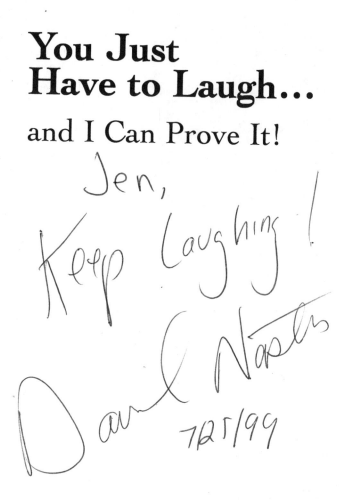

Jen,

Keep Laughing !

Dan C Nasters

7/25/99

Many people go through life wondering why they are put here. Some spend thousands of dollars on therapy, some climb mountains, and some try to save

the rainforest to make some sense out of life. Well, my friends, that is not David Naster. He has always known why he is here — to make people laugh!

I remember when I had my epiphany to become a comic. I stopped in at this comedy club, Stanford's and Sons in the Westport area of Kansas City. I asked this "guy," "How do I get a chance to perform on this stage?" He told me to come back the next week for Open Mic Night. That "guy" was David Naster.

I came back the next week and had the opportunity to watch this gifted comic at work. He was performing that night, so I stood in the back and watched him in awe. He turned the place out. He showed his energy and timing with drum sticks (you have to ask him about that one). He did material, he did improv, and he played music. I remember thinking, "Man, this guy is funny. I hope I can be that funny one day." I guess I had a good role model from the start.

We would later become friends and, sometimes, roommates. The thing that impressed me most about David was his confidence on stage and his love of comedy. So I stole those attributes from David (a comic has to steal something from a comic) and took them on the road with me.

Since my Kansas City days, I have had the opportunity to perform throughout the world and in front of all types of people. I have done movies, sitcoms, HBO specials, and other so-called cool things. But these things will never compare to the days of hanging out with my friend David Naster, talking about comedy, women, and counting the number of pieces of chicken in a bucket of Kentucky Fried Chicken.

I know that you are going to enjoy this book, just as I have enjoyed laughing with—and at—David.

Your friend,

Sinbad
P.S. Keep them laughing "Spanky"
(remember that one)

Acknowledgments

A Very Special Thank You To:

I first and foremost want to thank my good friend, Bob Gretz. My respect for him is of the highest regard. The depth of my appreciation is to let it be known that this book would not be what it is without Bob's integrity. Besides being my content editor and guidance counselor, he helped me focus this book.

Bob insisted I do the "heavy lifting" by putting everything together. Once completed, he and I went through every word, paragraph, and chapter—rewriting it to its purest form. Bob's keen insight and respect for my work made it a joyous collaboration.

I have realized as I have grown older that the greatest gift one person can give another is time. I thank Bob for his time as an editor, but I most thank him for being a true friend.

To my father, Howard, my brother, Mark, and Brad Plumb, thanks for helping during the early stages.

Thank you Denny Dey and Andy Smith for giving me all the juice and gas I needed to keep it moving.

I also wish to thank the Two West Inc. team: Dawn Grubb for bringing proper punctuation and clarity to this text; Brenda Clevenger for being my aggressive and reliable publicist; and Bart Herrman and Kris Flint for their excellent cover design and typesetting expertise.

Thanks To:

Thanks to Hank Young for taking the pictures and Danny Israel for making the tapes. Thanks to Lu Lu, "You kill me, Smalls." Thanks to my sister, Debbi; brother, Mike; Chris Wright; Sue Carper; Denny Anderson; Rick Wilgrubs; Elvy Rose; Bob Moore; Carl Peterson; Mike Murphy; Dan Hurst; Max, Tanna, and Moffit; Johnny Dare and Murphy; Dan, Glo, and Darci; Dan Church; Joyce Smith; Q-Networks Inc. and Nathaniel Pool for help with my Web page; and especially to everybody who contributed or said, "Here's a story for you."

One guy I want give a very special heartfelt thank you to is Tim Porter. Tim and I have been best friends for more than 30 years. His hours, days, and years of listening, encouragement, and keeping my rear in line is deeply appreciated. Our friendship runs deeper than any blood relation.

And finally, thanks to everybody who has ever done me wrong. Thanks to you, I have grown and have learned to laugh even more.

Dedication

First and foremost, I dedicate this book to my daughter, Rachel, who is my constant reminder of laughing and humor.

Second, to my parents, Howard and Louise Naster, for their never-ending support.

And finally, I dedicate this book to all of the original comedians in the world. Their **humorous perspective** makes us laugh and spreads its magic.

Table of Contents

Chapter 1
What's the Premise, Babe? .1

Chapter 2
Backed Into a Corner? 17

Chapter 3
The Fun House Mirror 31

Chapter 4
You Just Have to Laugh
At Your Family 45

Chapter 5
You Just Have to Laugh
At Yourself 61

Chapter 6
You Just Have to Laugh
At Your Job 75

Chapter 7
You Just Have to Laugh
At Your Job (Part 2: Public Service) 103

Chapter 8
You Just Have to Laugh
At Death 115

Chapter 9
You Just Have to Laugh
Even If You're Famous .133

Chapter 10
You Just Have to Laugh
And These People Prove It 151

Final Thoughts 169

Copyright © 1998 By David Naster.

Published by David Naster

Printed in the United States of America

First Printing March 1998

Second Printing October 1998

Library of Congress Card Catalog No.: 98-96060
ISBN No.: 0-9663145-0-6

Chapter 1

What's the
Premise, Babe?

For more than a year, I worked on this book without really knowing what I wanted it to be. Thoughts, ideas, paragraphs, stories ... all flew by in different directions. I felt like Dorothy in "The Wizard of Oz"; I wasn't sure where I was going to land. (I am a Kansas boy, you know.)

One day, I ran into an old comedian friend of mine, Mitchell Walters. Mitchell always had a way of helping me identify just what I wanted to do with a joke. He would listen to my thoughts and ideas, and then he would say, "What's the premise, babe?" From there, we would put together the words, gestures, and props that would turn my ideas into comedy routines.

So, in honor of Mitchell, that's what this first chapter is about.

The premise is simple: You just have to laugh. You just do. In this fast-paced, tension-filled world, there's only one sure-fire stress reducer—laughter. After a good laugh, we feel better physically, emotionally, and mentally. It works every time.

I've worked as a professional comedian for more than 20 years. That's how I've put bread on my table and a roof over my head. Creating laughter has been my only job.

But I was a comedian long before the IRS ever cared what I did for a living. As a kid, I used my wit and humor to diffuse tensions with family and friends. In high school, after performing in my first play, I was convinced that I wanted to be on stage the rest of my life. In college, it was the role of the court jester

Arlecchino in the play "The Venetian Twins" that convinced me I wanted to make people laugh.

My professional comedy career began as a mime and clown. I toured the world doing my one-man show in venues that ranged from city street corners to the prestigious Edinburgh Festival in Scotland. I moved on to stand-up comedy, where I developed my routines by warming up audiences at the cult movie "The Rocky Horror Picture Show."

I toured the country working college campuses, and for 10 consecutive years, I was nominated for National College Comedian of the Year. I won once. (So Susan Lucci, if you are reading this, there's still hope!) I graduated to comedy clubs around the country, eventually matriculated to the Comedy Store in Los Angeles. This was the comedy mecca in the 1980s, where I shared the stage with Robin Williams, Jerry Seinfeld, Richard Pryor, Eddie Murphy, Roseanne Barr (she had two names then), Jay Leno, and Gary Shandling.

I have created laughter in 48 of the 50 states. (I'm still waiting for bookings in New Hampshire and Vermont—call me, I'll cut you a special deal.) I have appeared on network and cable television shows too numerous to mention, and I hosted my own daily radio show.

I have learned to make people laugh—regardless of their age, sex, religious affiliation, or ethnic persuasion. It's the greatest job, and the best feeling in the world. (OK, so it may not be the best feeling in the world, but I'll leave that for you to decide.)

I have made many discoveries on my comedy quest. But one idea stands out above all else: You just have to laugh. Humor doesn't work without the laughter. That may seem obvious, but follow me on this line of thinking.

Humor is like the sense of smell. Think about the delicious aroma of fresh chocolate chip cookies when they are baking. That smell, without a doubt, is wonderful, inviting, and makes your mouth water like one of Pavlov's dogs. But if humor is the smell, then laughter is the actual tasting and eating of the cookies. Laughter is the gooey chocolate between your teeth and the cold glass of milk that washes down the cookie.

What I'm trying to say here is that nobody wants to just smell the cookies. We want to taste them. It's the same with humor and laughter. If you don't laugh, you miss the sweet taste of humor.

It was on a sunny Easter Sunday when I first learned the powerful combination of humor and laughter.

The scene was a small town in rural Kansas. I was performing in the town's largest church where every pew was filled with people who were laughing, thank God—no pun intended. The one routine that brought down the house involved a kazoo and a rather large man I selected from the congregation.

You know, the sound of a kazoo is just plain funny. What's even funnier is watching people struggle with that little instrument as they learn they must hum, not blow, to make that silly noise. When this gentleman finally figured out the trick, the sound of the kazoo filled the church and brought a thunderous response from the audience.

Once my new partner had mastered the kazoo, we went into the routine. We raced around the church as if we were riding motorcycles, communicating with each other only through the kazoos. By the time we were done, the congregation was howling. People were wiping away tears and holding their stomachs from laughing so hard. I thought that terrific show of appreciation would be my greatest reward that day.

I was wrong. After the show, I said my goodbyes and was a few feet outside the church heading toward my car when my kazoo-playing partner stopped me. He grabbed me by both shoulders, looked down at me and said, "Thank you."

I told him he was very welcome, but he still didn't release his grip on my shoulders.

"I mean it. Thank you," he said again.

At this point, the moment became extremely uncomfortable. Not only did he continue his near-crushing grasp on my shoulders, but tears were running down his face. His mouth quivered as he spoke softly, choosing his words carefully.

"I really want to thank you, Dave," he said. "You see, I lost my daughter about three months ago. This is the first time I've laughed since. I think I'm going to be all right. Thanks, partner."

He released his grip, patted me on the back, and walked away, wiping his eyes.

I'm not sure how long I stood there. I don't even remember him walking away. But his words touched the deepest part of my heart and soul. Since that moment, I have never taken for granted the magic, power, and value of laughing.

His words led me to another discovery—laughter can be a release. It eliminates the negatives that cause tension in our lives.

Imagine, if you will, the universe of a rubber band (courtesy of Rod Serling). When it's pulled, it becomes tight with tension. Release the rubber band, and it very powerfully moves back to a relaxed position.

That's exactly what humor and laughter do to tension in our lives. We get pulled tighter and tighter by the negatives. The instant release laughter brings **BOING**s the tension away, taking us back to a less stressful state.

BOING stands for:

Bounce Off Internal Negative Garbage.

Humor and laughter help remove negative thoughts and feelings and result in a release. Sometimes it's just a momentary release, but if you learn to lead your life with a smile, you'll have a skill that will last a lifetime.

I am always searching for the humor in life and the laughter that follows. You can find it around any corner and behind every door. One night, I was in a theater watching the movie "A Few Good Men," starring Jack Nicholson, Tom Cruise and Demi Moore. Right in the middle of the dramatic courtroom scene where Cruise goes after Nicholson, the screen went dark. There was that brief moment when everybody expected the movie to pop back on the screen. When it did not, there were a few catcalls as people were obviously getting irritated. After about 45 seconds of darkness, I decided to open the humor door and have some laughs. I stood up and asked, "OK, who has the remote control?"

Everyone in the theater laughed, and that broke the tension. I was basking in my comedy glory when the projectionist said over the sound system, "If Mr. Funny Man would please sit down, Tom Cruise would like to continue." That brought an even bigger laugh from the crowd, and I laughed the hardest at the projectionist's great line. (I probably should have left him a tip.)

What we both did was to **TOSS** a **humor grenade**

A **humor grenade** is something said or done that blows apart a tense situation, helping to diffuse it with laughter. **TOSS** stands for **Take Out Stressful Stuff.**

So the premise, babe, is that it all comes down to laughter removing the stress in our lives.

My friend, Art Crowell, knew that when he **TOSS**ed this **humor grenade.**

Art was a full colonel in the U.S. Army back in 1986. He was stationed at the Pentagon, where he took part in the budget meetings, which are an annual occurrence in military life. These meetings are held during several weeks, and they can become very stressful. Nerves become frayed as various branches of the military struggle to keep their allocations and programs.

On a cold February day, the meeting room was packed with about 50 heated military types, including many generals. They were all fighting to keep their programs in the face of severe budget cuts. One of those generals was Norman Schwartzkopf, who later became a household name when he headed up the Desert Storm operation.

On this day, Gen. Schwartzkopf was right on track toward earning his nickname "Stormin' Norman." As several of his programs were sliced from the budget, he was already at his boiling point. And then an aide delivered the message that he was about to lose even more funding. The reason? Another general needed a computer. Schwartzkopf went ballistic and began yelling at the top of his lungs.

"You are tearing the very guts out of this Army," he screamed. "How do you expect me to provide quality training for soldiers and officers when you take away my funds for a *&%$# computer?"

I'll let Art Crowell take it from here:

"Gen. Schwartzkopf was screaming at me, like it was all my fault. I remember looking at him, feeling his angry breath across the table, and doing my best to remain calm. When he finally came up for air, I smiled at him and said, 'Don't get mad at me; get mad at the messenger—and, by the way, I believe that messenger is dead!'

"There was not a sound in the room as all eyes turned toward the general. His reaction was immediate— he howled with laughter. Then everybody else began to laugh. You could feel the tension diminish as we got back to business solving the budget problems.

"After the meeting, Gen. Schwartzkopf slapped me on the back and said, 'Thanks, son, I needed that laugh. It made the rest of the meeting go a helluva lot better'."

Thank you Art Crowell for the **TOSS** of that **humor grenade**, and thank you Gen. Schwartzkopf for proving my point that when you laugh, you feel better. There's no room for anger, fear, or anxiety when you are laughing, because you're too busy enjoying yourself.

When you try this strategy, something magical happens to your perspective. Things that upset you before don't seem so bad. Problems, tensions, and conflicts appear less serious. That's what happens when you approach life with a **humorous perspective**.

Several years ago, a United Airlines pilot had to make an emergency landing in Sioux City, Iowa. The hydraulics system had failed on the DC-10 aircraft. Because he couldn't lower his landing gear or operate the flaps on the wings, a normal landing would be impossible.

As the plane circled the airport, the pilot and crew planned for the safest possible crash landing. During these tense moments, the folks in the control tower told him he could use any runway to land.

The pilot quickly answered back, "Oh, so you're going to be picky and make me use a runway?"

Here was a man in a life-or-death situation reacting with humor.

The plane never made it to a runway that day; it landed in a field near the airport. That more people did not perish in the crash was due to the pilot's skill and cool head. And I believe his **humorous perspective** helped.

Once you flick the humor switch, it puts a new light on everything. And everything doesn't have to be a crisis; even the mundane can become funny.

I've been visiting a friend's house for years, and every time I go over there his VCR is always flashing "12:00." I'm thinking he's either too lazy, or he can't figure out how to press a couple buttons. Either way, it makes me laugh.

Here are some other everyday things I find humor in:

- People who pull on doors when they are supposed to push—and push when they are supposed to pull.
- Watching someone open a can of soda that has been previously shaken.
- People who have treadmills, but also own riding mowers. Or, people who drive five blocks to use a stationary bike at a health club and then drive home.

Unpleasant situations in life can be laughed at as well. One time in Miami, my daughter, Rachel, and I had to make our way back to the cruise ship. It was a summer day with temperatures nearing 100 degrees and humidity pushing the area known as "Inferno." We had a three-mile walk ahead of us, one that would take us over a very tall, steep bridge.

Instead of walking, we decided to do the tango. We danced our way over this bridge. At first we smiled, then we giggled. A few hundred yards into it, we started laughing. Oh, we sweated a lot, but our silliness made us forget the distance. The time went by quickly, and I'm sure we gave the passing cars a good grin, as well.

When life's negatives overwhelm you, that's when humor should surface. For several years, I've been making presentations on the **humorous perspective.** One day in Dallas, I was explaining the big **BOING** theory by using a rubber band. During my talk, the rubber band broke.

There was a moment of uncomfortable silence, so I "grabbed" a **humor grenade** and said, "Oops— disgruntled postal worker."

There was some uncomfortable laughter from the audience. That's when the light bulb went off in my head; people who can't find the humor in life and laugh, those are the people who snap. (Thank God, my mailman is always smiling!)

It's like those buildings in California that actually move when there's an earthquake. They have flexibility. The quake comes and these buildings roll with the punches. It's the rigid buildings that come crashing down when the ground shakes.

When you laugh, you are more likely to bend

with the stresses and tensions of life. When your brain receives the signal that "something's wrong here," that's when the **humorous perspective** needs to take over. I call that moment the **jester reminder.** That's the time for a laugh.

The court jester's job was to make the king laugh, no matter the seriousness of the situation. He had to find humor, or he lost his head. The same goes for us. We have to let the **jester** inside of us do his job, so we don't lose our minds.

Dorthea Watson shows her **jester** all the time. Several years ago, I was working on a cruise ship when I met this lovely woman after one of my shows. She thanked me for making her laugh and told me how much she loved to laugh at life. This certainly appeared to be true, because throughout the cruise, every time I saw her, she was laughing. I asked her why she laughed all the time.

"You know, David, I'm 78 years old," she told me. "I laugh to either stay in a good mood or to get in one. I have arthritis, and when I laugh, my discomfort is gone. That's why I try to surround myself with humor."

There's the premise, babe. Laughing makes you feel better physically. If you don't want to believe me, there are laboratories and universities filled with researchers who have proven the connection.

"Laughing has an immediate impact on the body," says Dr. William Fry, a professor of psychiatry at Stanford Medical School. Fry has spent more than 40 years studying laughter's effect on the body and mind.

"The brain is stimulated into greater alertness and enhanced memory and sociability," Fry explains, adding that the immune system has been shown to be affected as laughter increases the concentration of circulating antibodies in the blood stream. This means a person is more resistant to developing infection.

"The stimulation of laughter increases our circulation because of its effect on the heart and blood pressure," Fry says. He explains that because laughter increases our respiratory exchange, with more oxygen coming in and more carbon dioxide going out, it also increases the metabolism and activity of our muscles.

"Laughing for 20 seconds gives the body the kind of workout you'd get from three minutes of rigorous exercise," according to Fry.

Perhaps the easiest to understand work on the effects of humor on the human body came from Norman Cousins. His best selling book, *Anatomy Of An Illness*, has been made into a television movie. He was diagnosed with a terminal illness and was given only a year to live.

But Cousins survived for more than 15 years thanks to his discovery that laughter was an integral part of the healing process.

"I made the joyous discovery that 10 minutes of genuine belly laughter had an anesthetic effect and would give me at least two hours of pain-free sleep," he wrote. "I call laughing inner jogging. When we engage in a good hearty laugh, every system in our body gets a workout.

"I see humor as food ... an adequate share of humor and laughter represents an essential part of the diet of the healthy person."

Humor and laughter provide nourishment, and they are available at any time of the day or night. It's like having 24-hour room service, and the good news is, you don't have to tip the waiter!

Laughter is free, there's an unlimited supply, and you have control over it. People say to me, "I'm not sure what I can laugh at anymore." That's a perfectly legitimate point. In these days of political correctness, one person's joke is another person's harassment. I think using political correctness is just another way of utilizing good manners. Should you think before you **TOSS** a **humor grenade**? Absolutely. Should your **jester** be aware of his surroundings before showing himself? Without a doubt.

Some people are wrapped pretty tight, and it's not your job to loosen them up. Making yourself laugh is the key. It's the only thing I take seriously anymore. If you have a **humorous perspective**, you have a shield from other people's negativity. As for those people who can't find their smile, I'm reminded of the words of Mark Twain:

"Against the assault of humor,
nothing can stand."

Within the pages of *You Just Have to Laugh* is a collection of stories from people who have lived Twain's words. They have made their way through life with a **humorous perspective** and have dealt with the mundane moments of their existence with a laugh. Others have amazed me by finding humor in some of life's greatest challenges. Whether they were concentration camp survivors, prisoners of war, or individuals suffering from devastating illnesses, these survivors somehow found solace in laughter.

Throughout this book, you will recognize people who understood the **BOING** theory and people who kept their **jester** on call at all times. You will read about people who have **TOSS**ed a **humor grenade** at some remarkable moments, never forgetting to use their 24-hour room service. For all of them, a **humorous perspective** was the guiding force in their lives.

As a comedian, I've always gone for the punch line. The people in this book lived the punch line. The best part of putting together these stories was the chance to laugh with them. I have laughed out loud too many times to count. (OK, it was 345 times.) I also shed some tears, but they came with a smile on my face.

I especially look forward to hearing you laugh, because, babe, that's the premise.

Chapter 2

Backed Into a Corner?

Have a TOSS and Laugh

"In prehistoric times, mankind often had
only two choices in crisis situations: fight
or flee. In modern times humor offers us
a third alternative: fight, flee—or laugh."

Roger Orben

How do you react when backed into a corner, a corner where there seems to be no escape or solution to a problem?

Do you find yourself confused, angry, even scared? Do you cry, scream, or pout? Not knowing how to resolve the situation, do you lash out at others, or do you completely shut down emotionally?

I'm here to tell you that every corner has an escape hatch. It's the humor door. Whether allowing the tension to **BOING** away, or blowing it up with the **TOSS** of a **humor grenade**, that helpless feeling can be dissolved with laughter.

That's what this chapter is all about—people laughing their way out of the challenging corners of life. They didn't ask, after the fact, "Do you know what I should have done?" or "Do you know what I should have said?" No, they simply worked their way out of that tight corner by using laughter as the key to opening the door with humor.

By doing so, they've taught us all a valuable lesson. Rather than fight or flee, we can laugh.

I'll start this chapter with a story of my own.

Hey, pretzel boy

After a performance at a comedy club in Springfield, Mo., I wanted to unwind and do some people watching before heading back to my hotel room. I stopped at an establishment that happened to be a country and western bar. It was one of those places with Merle Haggard on the jukebox, giant mugs of beer in every fist, and huge belt buckles at every waist.

I was standing at the bar, watching people have a good time, when two huge cowboys came up and stood on either side of me. They stood so close I knew something was about to happen. One guy looked at me and sneered, "Hey, pretzel boy." I'm not sure if you've seen the commercials on network television, but Jason Alexander (George Costanza on "Seinfeld") did a series of spots for a pretzel company. In these commercials he was called "pretzel boy." Obviously, this cowboy thought I resembled Jason Alexander. (Check out my picture on the book cover. What do you think?)

As he patted my bare forehead, he said, "You know what, pretzel boy? That feels like my old lady's butt. Do you know that?"

Although this was happening in the middle of the bar, I could feel myself backed into a corner. I had a real-life confrontation on my hands, and my options were few. One choice was to not say a word, walk off, and end up feeling humiliated. Or, I could throw the first punch at this cowboy—knowing for certain that it wouldn't be the last punch thrown that night. More than likely, I would then end up a hospital emergency room statistic.

That's why I chose a third option—**TOSS**ing a **humor grenade.** I began patting my forehead, then I said, "You're right. It does feel like your wife's butt!"

I laughed when I said it, and then—thank, God— the cowboys laughed, too, and smacked each other on the back. They got a big chuckle out of my **humor grenade.** The tension was gone. They invited me to share a beer with them. I told them I would after I used the restroom. Leaving them laughing, I headed for the exit and never looked back.

I had scored a direct hit with that **TOSS.**

Now for some other **humor grenades.** The first one is about a couple who shall remain nameless, because their identity is not what's important to this story.

Is there humor in divorce?

In the middle of an extremely tense and difficult divorce, the husband returned to the house that would soon belong to his ex-wife. He wanted to remove the last of his possessions.

The wife was having a difficult time getting through the divorce. Her husband had been unfaithful, and when confronted with his infidelity, he asked for the dissolution of the marriage.

After he had gathered up the last of his belongings and was heading for the door, he turned around, looked at his soon to be ex-wife and with the utmost sincerity said:

"I know this has been difficult for you. Believe me, it's been difficult for me, too. But, do you think after this is all over, we could still have sex?"

She looked at him in amazement and shock. But rather than lash out, she allowed her **jester** to rise up and hand her a perfect **TOSS**.

Smiling, she said, "Sure we can continue to have sex ... but not with each other!"

With the smile still on her face, she leaned forward and slammed the front door in his face. Later, she told friends that moment of laughter helped her begin to move on.

Bats on a subway

A fellow comedian had just finished a late-night comedy performance at a club in midtown Manhattan. He had another appearance that evening in Greenwich Village. Anyone who has been to New York knows how hard it is to get around that part of Manhattan, especially in the middle of the night. He thought about taking a cab, but the fare would have cost him nearly all the money he had just made. So he decided to take the subway.

The New York subways can be a dangerous place at night, so the comedian was relieved to find he was the only passenger in his subway car. That feeling didn't last long, however, as six punk rockers came barging in, laughing, and making a lot of noise with their military boots.

They had torn clothing, multicolored mohawk haircuts, and faces pierced in enough places to make them look like fishing lures. Plus, they all carried baseball bats.

As the train rumbled out of the station, the entire group began banging their bats on the floor and seats. When they noticed the comedian sitting in the corner, they stopped and stared at him. The roar of the subway contrasted with the deafening silence inside the car.

All eyes were on him. Looking past their intimidating facial expressions, their anger-filled body language, and their enormous baseball bats, the comedian threw out his line.

"Big game tonight, fellows?"

They laughed. He not only laughed—he lived, too. Thanks to his **humor grenade**, it all worked out.

I'm sleeping here

Comedian Richie Minnervini was pulled over by the police in Long Island, N.Y. According to a tip, he fit the description of a guy who was selling narcotics. The police asked him to get out of the car. When they told him they thought he was dealing drugs, he said, "You can't stop me because you think I'm selling dope. That would be as stupid as arresting me because I'm thinking about punching out both of you."

In this case, Richie did not correctly judge his audience. He was handcuffed and in the back seat of the patrol car in a matter of seconds. Upon arriving at the detention center, Richie was handed a blanket and pillow and taken to a large holding cell, which was filled with some of New York's finest thugs. After he returned from making his one phone call, his pillow and blanket were gone.

Just a little bit mad at himself, and with his nerves that were more than a little bit rattled by the events of the evening, Richie screamed, "Whoever took my blanket and pillow, I want them back now!"

A man the size of a building stepped forward and said, "I've got what you want. So what are you going to do about it?"

Understand, Richie is all of 5 feet 6 inches tall and maybe 160 pounds. But his **humorous perspective** is much bigger. In a serious tone, he looked up at the man and said, "Give them back to me now, because if I don't get them back, somebody is going to get his butt kicked—and it's probably going to be me."

There was a second of silence before everyone understood. That's when the laughter started. The big guy was the last to get it, but even he laughed and said, "Here's your blanket, but I'm keeping the pillow."

In this case, Richie's first **humor grenade** was a bit off the mark. But like all people with their **jester** ready, he was undaunted and his second **TOSS** hit the bull's-eye.

Sometimes there are people in life who don't see

the humor in anything. That's when you know it's time to move on to others. Using your unique humor may be your passport to a brighter and quicker freedom.

Oh my God, she's a Jamaican

Patrick Murray is a master ventriloquist. He's 6 feet 2 inches tall, and white. The puppet he uses in his act is a black Jamaican puppet named Matilda. And Patrick's Jamaican accent is so authentic that Jamaicans enjoy Matilda's character more than anyone.

Here are Patrick's own words:

"One time, I was going through customs in Montego Bay when a Jamaican official, looking through my bags, saw a couple of the puppet heads and said in a fearful voice, 'Oh my God, this is something bad.'

"I immediately explained I was a ventriloquist, but the man did not understand. After 15 minutes of getting nowhere, I finally reached into the bag, pulled out Matilda, put her right in front of the official, and said in a perfect Jamaican accent, 'Hello, my darling.'

"The customs official stepped back and said, 'Oh my God, she's Jamaican.' Matilda and the customs official continued to have a full-blown conversation, never realizing it was me talking the entire time.

"Finally, Matilda called the customs official closer and said, 'You see this big white guy behind me? He knows some bad, wicked voodoo.' I was through customs in a matter of seconds."

After these past few stories, you might think you have to be a professional comedian or entertainer to fight your way out of a corner with humor and laughter. That's not the case, as these next stories illustrate.

Honk, if you're an idiot

It happened during the afternoon rush hour in a city notorious for its traffic jams, Houston. Shirley was in the middle lane of the expressway traffic, and she was stuck. Her car had died.

Shirley kept turning the key, but all she heard was a clicking sound. At the time, she did not have a clue what was wrong, but her battery was dead. Because of that, there was no air conditioning and her power windows would not go down. It just happened to be one of the hottest days of the summer—103 degrees to be exact. Like they say down in Texas, "It might have been cooler on the sun that day."

It didn't take long before Shirley felt like a Thanksgiving turkey. That's when she heard the first honk. A man in the car behind her was hotter than the pavement, and he was laying on his horn. In her rear-view mirror, Shirley could see him screaming at her. His windows were up, and his air conditioner was obviously working, but it was pretty warm in his car, too.

Frustrated, hot, and now angry, Shirley reached her boiling point. She got out of the car, walked back and knocked on Mr. Honker's window. He froze for a second and then slowly lowered the glass.

As a rush of cold air hit Shirley in the face, she said, "You know, I'll be glad to get into your nice cool, functioning automobile and honk your horn, if you would care to get out and start my car."

He laughed; then Shirley laughed. He invited her to wait in his car while he called a road service on his cellular phone.

In this day of "road rage," wouldn't it be nice if everybody on the highway would just chill and take a laugh. As Shirley found out in this case, it's a far cooler thing to **BOING** that tension away.

Pull over

A woman was speeding down an interstate highway in Oklahoma. Cars were passing her left and right, so she figured she wouldn't get a ticket. Much to her surprise, she was stopped by a highway patrolman.

The policeman asked her, "Do you know why I pulled you over?"

She quickly responded, "Yeah, I was the only one you could catch."

The policeman laughed and let her go without a ticket.

Next in line, please

Here's another place where people always seem to be tense—airports.

Jim McNut worked in the baggage department at American Airlines in Kansas City. It was his job to help people locate their lost luggage.

One day, as he was filling out the necessary paperwork to retrieve missing baggage, a man began cursing at Jim, threatening to sue both him and the airline. The man said the lost bag was going to cost him a day's work, and he blamed Jim personally for this inconvenience.

A line was forming behind the man, but Jim kept his cool, reassuring the man he would be able to track down the bag. But the man became increasingly indignant, and soon the volume of his profane language matched that of the jet engines outside.

It was then that Jim **BOING**ed the tension away. Calmly he said, "Twenty minutes ago, sir, there were two people concerned about your lost luggage. Now, there's only one. Next in line, please!"

Everyone behind the man laughed, and Jim quietly moved on to help other travelers.

He doesn't know who he is

A United Airlines flight was canceled. The agent at the ticket counter was handling a long line of irritated people. Most managed to keep some semblance of composure, save one.

This man pushed and butted his way to the front of the line. He slapped his ticket down on the counter and yelled, "I have to be on the next flight, and it has to be in first class!"

Without raising her voice, the agent said, "I'm sorry, sir, I'll be happy to try and help you, but these folks in line were here first. As soon as I take care of them, I'll be glad to help you."

The man yelled back, loud enough so everybody in line could hear, "Do you have any idea who I am?"

With that, the ticket agent grabbed the microphone and announced over the terminal's public address system: "Attention, please. We have a passenger here at the gate who doesn't know who he is. If anyone can help him identify himself, please come to the gate."

The people in line began to laugh. The man gritted his teeth and swore, "#!?* you."

The agent kept her cool and said, "I'm sorry, sir, but you'll have to wait in line for that, too."

The man retreated, as the rest of the line laughed hysterically and applauded.

That ticket agent knew that a well **TOSS**ed **humor grenade** allows you to avoid or diffuse most confrontations.

Blue ribbon

It was in San Diego one night that a group of people attending a convention went out to dinner. Leroy Markee was part of this group. As a host of the convention, Leroy was wearing a name tag with a red ribbon that read "Sponsor."

Understand that Leroy is a good old boy from Odessa, Texas, who definitely looks at life with a **humorous perspective.** So, rather than wear his name tag on his shirt, he stuck it over his belt buckle.

As he walked toward his party, Leroy passed a table crowded with Marines enjoying a night on the town. Noticing the tag on his buckle, one of them commented loudly, "Nice ribbon."

Leroy looked down and realized he had forgotten to remove the name tag. Turning toward the Marines, he smiled and said, "Gentlemen, if the good Lord would have blessed me just a little bit more, I would have gotten the blue ribbon." The entire table of Marines erupted with laughter.

The best part of Leroy's story is what he told the folks at his own table when he finally got there.

"Yeah," he said, "I just **TOSS**ed one of those **humor grenades** the guy was talking about this morning."

You see, I had given my Humorous Perspective Seminar to his group earlier that day. Thanks for listening, Leroy, and enjoy the laughter.

Chapter 3

The Fun House Mirror

Exaggerate...
Exaggerate...
Exaggerate...

> "The ability to be outrageous is what helps
> you live. People suffer from terminal seri-
> ousness. We can reverse that."
>
> *Dr. Robert Charm*

Remember that silly fun house mirror at the car-
nival? Remember how you laughed as it distorted your
features, making you look 7 feet tall, or 7 feet wide, or
turning your face into a twisted mask?

The fun house mirror exaggerates our features to
the point of being ridiculous. In times of conflict and
tension, humor and laughter do the same thing. By
placing the **fun house mirror** in front of the problems
and challenges in your life, you can enjoy the distorted angle it provides. Instead of gritting your teeth and
churning your stomach when the stress level goes up,
you may even find yourself chuckling.

Take the trip my daughter, Rachel, and I made on
an open-air pleasure boat in the British Virgin Islands.
Our group's destination was a small island where we
were going to do some snorkeling. The boat ride was
scheduled to take one hour.

But along the way, we encountered some rough
seas, and, after an hour, we weren't even halfway
there. Since we were all sitting outside, we were
soaked and there was not a dry towel to be found.
Some people were getting seasick, and despite the
tropical sun, Rachel was cold.

I attempted to distract her by singing Christmas
carols, even though it was the middle of March. She

joined in. So did our friend, Jeffrey, and it didn't take long for our boat to turn into a drenched but melodic Caribbean chorus.

It was our look into the **fun house mirror** that allowed us to get through what could have been a miserable day. With a **humor perspective**, exaggeration becomes easy.

"Live long, die short"

"I'm 66, but I don't look a day older than 65."

That was Bob Charm's first comment over the phone. He didn't stop there.

"I even dye my hair gray to look old."

That's Robert M. Charm, M.D. He created his "Foundation for Good Health" to teach people how to "live long and die short."

Dr. Charm has been practicing medicine for more than 30 years. He's a doctor of internal medicine, specializing in gastroenterology. He has a private practice in the San Francisco Bay area, and he's one of the few doctors around who still makes house calls.

"I have a theory that's even better than Einstein's," he said. "Einstein had E=mc2, but I have **Five E's=LQL. "**

"My five E's are **Eat, Enjoy, Educate, Exercise** and **Eliminate.** Combine those and they equal **Long Quality Life.**

"One of my good friends was Norman Cousins and, like him, I believe that being happy, enjoying yourself, and laughing are the key ingredients to a quality life," Dr. Charm said.

He even wrote a poem that summarizes his view on life. "I gave it to the governor of Arkansas in 1992, and I told him to read it and he would be elected president," Dr. Charm said. "Obviously, he read it, so now I call it the No. 1 poem in America."

You may not know it;
But you're a poet,
A magician, a musician,
A work of art.
So laugh and smile often,
It will life's trials soften.
Eat, exercise, eliminate, educate,
And enjoy each day.
Be outrageous;
Good health is contagious.

Bob Charm made me laugh. I felt rejuvenated and happy for hours after our conversation. I wanted to share this "Shaman of Humor" because I realized that humor is like charm. It can wiggle you out of stressful situations, especially when you are as wonderfully out-rageous and exaggerated as the good Dr. Charm.

Level 10 laughs

As these stories show, putting your problems in front of the **fun house mirror** can make living life less painful.

The Midwest Rehabilitation Hospital is located in Overland Park, Kan. One of the hospital's biggest programs involves teaching people how to manage and control chronic pain.

I was asked to speak at the chronic back pain clinic. It was there that I met Michael, who lived with constant and, sometimes, debilitating back pain. During the previous weekend, Michael had experienced pain that reached level 10.

In the world of pain, there is a scale to measure its intensity. It ranges from 1, which is considered no pain, to the highest level of 10, the most serious. The measuring is done through bio-feedback devices.

I'll let Michael take the story from here:

"I was trying to find something to take my mind off the pain, so I started channel surfing on the television. I came across the movie "48 Hours" with Eddie Murphy and Nick Nolte.

"As I watched the movie, I started laughing and my focus shifted away from the pain. Minutes later, when I checked my pain it had dropped down to a level 6.

"The laughing definitely distracted me from my pain."

Dr. Jim Lemon, who works at the hospital, is a nationally known expert in stress psychology and pain management. He explained to the group how Michael's laughter had led to a reduction in his pain. Then Dr. Lemon introduced me, mentioning that I was a comedian, but also pointing out that I was researching the positive aspects of humor.

My first one-liner—"Hi, I'm David, and I'm an alcoholic. Oops, wrong meeting."— brought a surprisingly loud laugh, so I was encouraged to continue speaking for about five minutes, counting on my sure-fire funny stuff to keep them all laughing.

Then I decided to try turning the **fun house mirror** on their pain. I asked the group for reasons it's good to be at level 10. Suddenly, the room was silent. I doubt they had ever associated their misery with humor. Dr. Lemon glanced at me with a curious look on his face. If he was wondering what the outcome might be, he wasn't alone. I had no idea how they would react either.

But luckily, they peeked in the **fun house mirror.**

"No responsibility," yelled out one man.

"You get to sleep all day," said a woman.

Michael blurted out, "Twenty-four hour room service."

"More drugs," was the response that caused an eruption of laughter in the room.

Everybody was getting involved, and with each response, the laughter grew louder. People who earlier were frowning were now laughing. The woman who was in too much pain to sit up at the beginning of the meeting was now perched on the edge of her chair. Even an elderly gentlemen laying on the floor with a pillow under his back was blurting out responses.

The **fun house mirror** created a great moment; they realized they could laugh at their arch enemy, pain.

Top ten? Top this

I work with many school districts throughout the United States, sparking students' creativity through the use of humor. One method I use teaches them to create their own Top 10 lists, much like David Letterman does on his late-night television show.

Top 10 lists often spring from issues that might be considered controversial or sensitive, giving students the freedom to use humor and exaggeration to poke fun at subjects that are usually very serious.

Here are some of the lists that a class of fifth-graders came up with.

Things You Don't Say at the Thanksgiving Table:
- I like this turkey. By the way, have you seen the cat?
- Did you know dog hair is flammable?
- Mom, hasn't this cranberry stuff been in the refrigerator since August?
- Dad, isn't this the dressing you accidentally sneezed on?
- Grandma, your teeth are in the wine.

Reasons Not to Fall Down on the Playground:
- The family lawyer is on vacation.
- I wouldn't want to miss any exciting education.
- I might rip jeans, and that style went out last year.
- I might have to visit school nurse, and she smells.

Excuses for Not Having Homework Done:
- I'm allergic to paper.
- I start getting rashes when I hear the word "homework."
- I don't know what homework means.
- I had to go somewhere.
- I forgot I had school.
- I forgot where I lived.
- I forgot where the school was.
- Where am I now?

The teachers who sent me these lists included this note:

"The students had an absolute blast writing these lists. The room was alive and full of enthusiasm. What a great way to bust up cabin fever. Some kids want to do this every week, and they are even bringing in their own suggestions for subjects."

These kids reminded me of one of my favorite quotes. It comes from author Robert Burton in his book *Anatomy of Melancholy:*

"Mirth is the principal engine for battering the walls of melancholy."

Think you're funny, Mr. Funny Man?

Comedian Jeff Zerbrowskie was working at a club in Long Island, N.Y. During his show, Jeff had some fun with an Italian guy, making a few cracks about the possibility of the guy being a member of the Mafia. There were a lot of Italians in the audience, and they seemed to find the comedy highly entertaining.

The next day, the object of Jeff's attention called. Here's how the conversation went:

Man: Hey, Mr. Funny Guy, I didn't appreciate those jokes you made about me and the Mafia last night.

Jeff: Oh yeah, I thought they were pretty funny, and obviously the audience did too.

Man: Well, hey, Milton Berle, how's about I send my boys over to take care of you.

Jeff: Boys?

Man: Yeah, funny guy, my boys.

Jeff: How many boys?

Man: As many as it takes. Would you like to meet my boys? They'd shut your big mouth up.

Jeff: If these boys are fifth- or sixth-graders, I can take a bunch of them.

Man: Hey, funny man, my boys would mess you up.

Jeff: What are you hanging around all these boys for? There are laws against that.

Man: You meet my boys, you won't be laughing so hard.

Jeff: Well that depends how big and how many

... and, hey, when did you start hanging around playgrounds?

The guy hung up because he started to laugh. Thanks to the **fun house mirror** nobody "sleeps with the fishes."

A needed distraction

One day, novelist Arthur C. Clarke was reading a newspaper when he saw a story he wanted to share with his friends.

"During a crash landing of a commercial airliner, one passenger in the story had been quoted as saying, 'I was reading an Arthur C. Clark novel, and it took my mind off the potential disaster.'

"After the story was printed, I sent clippings of it to all of my pals, including one of my dearest friends, the late, great science-fiction author Isaac Asimov. I included this note:

Dear Isaac,

If only he would have been reading one of your novels, he would have slept through the whole thing."

Joyous noise

As rector in an Episcopalian church, Father Terrance C. Roper understands the congregation's anxiety when it comes to the business affairs of the church. The need for more funds is never an easy subject to discuss. Keeping that in mind, Father Roper approached his flock with this during one of his Sunday sermons:

"It is time now to make a joyous noise unto the Lord," Father Roper said. "Now remember, the Lord can clearly hear this joyous noise—and the Lord wants to hear this joyous noise.

"You all look confused. Allow me to explain. What is that joyous noise? Why, that joyous noise is simply the glorious sound of hundreds of checks being simultaneously ripped from your checkbooks."

It was a l-o-n-g journey

Chuck Bridwell is the minister of music at the University Baptist Church of Coral Gables, Fla. Each year, he directs the Miami Christmas Pageant, which is held in the 2,400-seat Dade County Auditorium. All eight performances are sold out every year.

The cast numbers more than 400 people and includes live animals. There are camels for the three wise men, sheep for the shepherds, and a donkey for Mary and Joseph to use on their journey to Bethlehem.

I'll let Chuck take the story from here:

"One year, our seasoned donkey died, so we were forced to find another one. Our animal trainer found a replacement, but this donkey had never been on stage before. Our last dress rehearsal was a bit shaky; however, the new donkey managed to successfully carry Mary, with Joseph by her side, across the stage.

"On opening night, the time came for Mary and Joseph to make their journey to Bethlehem. With Mary on its back, the donkey came about 15 feet on stage, stared up at the spotlight, and started backing up toward the painted hills of Judea. When his rear end touched the backdrop, he froze.

"I was on the headset yelling for the lighting director to cut the spotlight. A few more actors joined Joseph in trying to encourage the donkey to complete his journey across the stage. When the spotlight was finally cut, the regular stage lights revealed a half-dozen actors pulling the donkey across the stage, a very shaken Mary still clinging to his back.

"That's when the narrator delivered his next line, which brought a roar of laughter and applause.

"'Yes, it was a l-o-o-o-o-ng journey to Bethlehem,'" he said.

Hold that plane

Being "outrageous" can bring a lot of laughter. Include exaggeration, and that's what the **fun house mirror** is all about. This final story is the perfect example.

An America West plane had left the gate at the Sky Harbor Airport in Phoenix right on time. In fact, it had been gone for a full 15 minutes when a man came running through the terminal, screaming at the top of his lungs: "Hold that plane! Hold that plane!"

As he skidded to a halt in front of the gate's ticket counter, he asked the women working there, "Where's the plane?"

The counter agent said calmly, "Which one?"

The man pointed at the spot where the plane had been and said, "That one!"

"I'm sorry, sir," replied the ticket agent. "That plane is gone."

"Where was it headed?"

"Los Angeles."

"Did it leave on time?"

"Yes."

The man stood there for a second and then demanded that the ticket agent call the pilot. When she asked him why, he said he wanted to speak to the pilot so he could bring the plane back to the gate.

The ticket agent picked up the phone and acted as if she was talking to the pilot.

She asked urgently, "Where are you? Oh you are in the air ... and you are just now at 30,000 feet. Can you get back? You are sure of that? There's a man here that really wants to be on that plane. Oh, you can't."

She put her hand over the phone and asked the man what she should do now.

The man said, "Just tell him to go on."

The ticket agent said goodbye to the imaginary pilot and then booked the man on the next flight.

He was laughing as he walked away.

Chapter 4

You Just Have to Laugh... At Your Family

If Blood is Thicker Than Water, Then I Need a Transfusion

"Your sense of humor will be your best
weapon."

Louise and Howard Naster

I have two wonderful parents who taught me the
power of humor. They did it simply by living every
day with a **humorous perspective.**

Whether it was Dad's constant jokes, or Mom's
joyous approach to each day, they made our home a
place for fun and laughter. They also taught me that I
would meet negative and mean-spirited people along
the way. Mom's advice was, "Keep a cool head, a
humorous attitude—and get away from those people
as fast as you can."

They practiced what they preached. Traveling
with a tour group in Italy, one of their companions
turned out to be a grumpy old man who was rude and
mean to everyone. One day, the group was in a bak-
ery, and Mom ordered a bagel. Mr. Grumpy said curt-
ly, "You don't need a bagel, you're too fat already."

Without blinking, Mom said, "Oh, thank you for
telling me. I am so relieved. All these years, I thought
I was pregnant."

Mr. Grumpy did not have a comeback. Mom disarmed him with her **humor grenade.** (She also didn't
share a breakfast table with him that morning.)

Later during the trip, this same man said to my
father, "I have a rug that looks just like that shirt
you're wearing." Dad looked at him, smiled, and said,
"That must be some expensive rug."

That's Mom and Dad!

As you can see, I grew up in a family that constantly kept their **jester** at their side. At an early age, I learned to look at situations and use humor to skew the picture. That's what everyone in my family did, and we haven't stopped.

At a recent family gathering, we were laughing over some expressions we wished our parents would have said when we were growing up. Like:

- Don't wipe that smile off of your face!
- Slouch as much as you want.
- Eat the ice cream, forget the brussel sprouts!
- Come home as late as you want.
- Stay home from school tomorrow; you look tired.

For the most part, the list was created by Mom and Dad.

My parents' **humorous perspectives** have been handed down to their eight grandchildren. I would like to introduce you to one of them. He's my nephew, Shane Naster.

Shane suffers from McCune-Albright Syndrome. There are fewer than 100 people in the country who have this malady. A McCune-Albright diagnosis requires the patient have two of the following conditions:

1. Bones turn into fibrous tissue, deteriorate, break, and deform.
2. Puberty begins and ends earlier than normal.
3. Birthmarks cover the body.

Shane has dealt with all three of these conditions. He has undergone seven major operations, four of

which ended with a body cast, and his diseased bones are held together with rods and plates. When the pain in his legs becomes too severe, he gets around by using a wheelchair.

This continual pain throughout his young life has not broken his humorous spirit or extinguished his ability to laugh.

One time he called me and said, "Make me laugh Uncle David. I just had a biopsy. Do you know what a biopsy is, Uncle David?"

I said to him, "Isn't that a new flavor of yogurt? I heard it tastes like root beer."

Shane giggled. "No, Uncle David, it's like an operation."

"You say you went to the opera? I didn't know you liked the opera," I replied.

"No, Uncle David, it's an operation," he said with a laugh.

"You ate yogurt at the opera?"

"You're funny, Uncle David," Shane said.

The fact that Shane was able to laugh at my silliness so soon after a painful biopsy delighted me. But his willingness to unleash his **jester** at McCune-Albright astonishes me.

There was the day he was cut open for an operation and then sewn back up because the doctor brought the wrong hardware to put in his legs. When Shane was told what had happened, he said, smiling, "Oh boy, another day without a body cast."

One day Shane broke his arm and had to suffer

through long, grueling hours undergoing X-rays and waiting to get his arm set. On the way home from the hospital he told his mother, "Well, I had a pretty good day today, except I broke my arm."

When he watches other kids run, jump, and play sports, he quips, "I could do that. My mom just won't let me."

Sometimes I feel sorry for Shane, but his perspective quickly chases those thoughts away. I'll always remember a comment he made when his family pulled up to an amusement park.

"See, Grandma, it's not so bad being handicapped," said Shane. "It's kind of cool how they always move me up to the front of all the long lines, and look, we get to park in the front row of the parking lot, too."

This chapter is about families laughing together. It's about parents and children finding the humor in life's twists and turns. A **humorous perspective** may be the greatest gift a parent can offer a child.

Please indulge me, as I share with you another story from the Naster family album.

Could be worse ... could be raining

My brother, Mark's, family loves watching funny movies. One of their favorites is Mel Brooks' "Young Frankenstein." There is a scene where actors Marty Feldman, as Igor, and Gene Wilder, as Dr. Frankenstein, are digging up a grave. With the only light coming from a weak lantern, they struggle through the dirt and heat to rob the grave. In the middle of their frustration, Igor says, "Could be worse. Could be raining." At that moment, a downpour starts.

I'll let Mark take it from here:

"We're always using that phrase around the house. When anyone notices another family member down or frustrated, they'll say, 'Could be worse.' and always, someone will blurt out, 'Could be raining.' and we all share a laugh.

"My daughter, Jaclyn, was in the middle of a soccer match, and her team was losing badly. I watched her frustration and yelled from across the field, 'Could be worse.'

Her head came right up, and she smiled, yelling back, 'Could be raining.'

At the game the following week, Jaclyn's team was getting beat again, this time on a drizzly, miserable day.

'Could be worse,' I hollered.

She yelled back with a laugh, 'It is raining, Dad!'"

I'm expecting a call from the doctor

Comedian Rich Purpura was working on a cruise ship that docked in Key West, Fla. He hurried off the ship so he could call his pregnant wife, Pam, at home in Youngstown, Ohio. He had no more than said "hello," when Pam said, "Call me back in 15 minutes. I'm expecting a call from the doctor."

Rich's 15-minute wait seemed like an eternity. When he called back, Pam told him there was nothing to worry about. I'll let Rich continue the story:

"My adorable pregnant wife was getting ready to take her prenatal pills. At the same time, she was about to give our dog, Elroy, his heart worm pills. Somehow, she ended up taking Elroy's heart worm pills instead of her prenatal pills. She called the doctor to see if she or the baby was in any danger. The doctor told her they would both be fine.

"Then I asked her if she gave Elroy the prenatal pills.

"Pam answered, 'What do you think I am, stupid?'"

What's up doc?

Sally Balot thought she was suffering from the early effects of Alzheimer's disease. She asked her grandson, Rich, to take her to the family doctor for a diagnosis. Rich told me what happened:

"The thought of getting Alzheimer's really scared my grandmother. When we got to the doctor's office, she explained to him her recent forgetfulness and her fear of losing her memory. She asked the doctor what she should do.

"The doctor paused a moment, looked at her, and said, 'I'd just forget about it.'

"I couldn't believe what he had said. Grandma and I were both speechless. Then, I saw him smile. Then Grandma laughed.

"The doctor reassured her she was fine and that she had nothing to be concerned about. His ability to make Grandma laugh was just what she needed to forget about it."

We're not supposed to do that

This story was told to me by a man who requested we change the names to save his hide at the next family reunion. He said, "Sometimes it takes a child's view to refocus our **humorous perspective.**"

"Uncle Glenn is a World War II veteran who had his leg amputated because of diabetes. He's a crusty old sort and was getting grumpier by the day. The family purchased a prosthesis for him, but in his stubbornness, he refused to wear it.

"One day, Glenn and his son, Ralph, were sitting in the kitchen. They were having a heated discussion on his refusal to wear the prosthesis, which was lying on the table. One of Glenn's grandsons walked in and saw the fake leg. Sensing the tension in the room, the grandson said, 'Hey, Grandpa, take your foot off the table. You know we're not supposed to do that.'

"His comment not only made Ralph laugh out loud, but even Uncle Glenn chuckled. I'm not sure if that did it, but soon after, he began to wear his prosthesis."

We laughed till we cried ... then we laughed some more

Denny Dey is a very successful storyteller and motivational speaker. He told me his **humorous perspective** developed very early in life. Take it away, Denny:

"My parents were married, divorced, remarried, then divorced again. The only ones enjoying all this were their attorneys. To keep our sanity, my big brother and I would flee the house, escaping to the local high school. We would sit in the sand of the long jump pit and re-enact all the fighting we had just heard.

"We would exaggerate their voices, change parts, and be outrageously silly. We would make ourselves laugh until we cried. I'm grateful that for whatever reason, I chose to laugh about it and that my big brother and I had each other as an audience.

"Even today, I tell people if they are sick and tired of being sick and tired, just laugh."

He rose to the occasion

There are other families where parents and children laugh at their troubles together. I met Rebecca and Al Somodevilla and their son, Paul, on a cruise ship. They caught my attention when I heard them laughing from across a busy lounge. I asked if I could join them, and they shared with me their family's **humorous perspective**.

Paul was a senior in high school. During a rehearsal for the senior talent show, he fell 15 feet into the orchestra pit. He fractured major facial bones and tissue and lost a lot of teeth. His doctor compared his injuries to those of someone who goes through the windshield of a moving car.

Two days later at the talent show performance, to the surprise of everyone, Paul limped on stage. His voice was barely audible because his mouth was wired shut, but Paul grabbed the microphone and said, "If you think a little fall would stop me from being here, then you must be smoking something."

The audience was on its feet with a roaring ovation. Later that year in the senior review, the show began with Paul crawling out of the orchestra pit, asking when the talent show started. Another standing ovation.

Speaking of his son, Al Somodevilla told me, "Paul talked to me after his fall. He thought it must have happened for a reason and that reason was so he would learn to laugh and go on. As a psychiatrist, I was impressed. As his father, I couldn't have been prouder. He continues to have fun with his fall by joking around with his false teeth. He is an amazing young man and an inspirational son."

Al thinks the family's ability to laugh runs deep in their blood. He points to his Grandma Pilar, who fled Castro's Cuba to start over in the United States. Along the way, she lost two sons and a husband, but she was never depressed, according to Al.

"Even at 82 years old she was playing poker with the other patients in the nursing home, winning money, and laughing about it," Al said. "Her attitude was, 'In life we have several choices. If you choose to be miserable, people will shun you and not be around you. If you decide to laugh, you will have more friends than you ever thought possible'."

Al's wife, Rebecca, added, "Humor is a temporary bridge until you can face your conflicts head on. Then it's also your highway away from them."

One day, while Rebecca was working as a registered nurse, a man died in the emergency room. It was busy in the emergency room that day, so the man's body was constantly being moved from place to place. Every time Rebecca turned around, she saw the body. It was eventually wheeled into Rebecca's office where she was on the phone trying to find the man's next of kin.

"It actually got to be funny, because no matter where I went, he was there," said Rebecca. "By the end of the day I just wanted to go home, but I couldn't until I located his family. I called Al and told him we might have a dinner guest that evening. I found myself laughing with him about the possibilities of dining with a dead man. What a day! I couldn't have gotten through it without laughing.

"The greatest humor comes from the greatest pain. Laughter is very insulating and protective, so no matter what happens, you have to laugh about it."

The spirit of '76

John Schuler's grandmother was a special woman. She raised John's father by herself during the Depression. She went to college when she was in her 60s and became a highly sought-after speaker on the subject of the history of St. Louis, Mo.

By the time an extended illness forced her into a nursing home, her mind was no longer sharp, and her attention would drift. She would tell some pretty wild stories, which her family knew were not true. It was hard for John and his family to visit Grandma because her condition scared and saddened them.

I'll let John continue:

"One day, when my oldest sister and I were visiting Grandma, we asked her how she felt. She said she was tired. I asked her why, and she started one of her stories. 'Well, I've been up all night dancing,' Grandma said. 'They're putting on a talent show here, and we have to practice. They made us practice all night. I told them I wanted to go to bed, but they made me practice, and I danced all night. I'm tired, but the show must go on.'

"My sister started to cry, but I said, 'You're a real trooper Grandma!' My sister looked at me like 'What are you doing?' But I'd decided to play along with Grandma's fantasy this time.

"As Grandma started another story, my sister decided to play along as well. Our interest just added more spark to her fiery stories. When we left the room, we laughed. As a matter of fact, we laughed all the way home. Later, we told the rest of the family what we had done. I told them I thought there was no reason to correct her and that I thought we should just go along with her stories and make it fun for her, and us.

"My family took this advice, and the humor eased our sadness. Her final year, she boasted about being 76 years old, like the spirit of '76. That was her claim to fame—she was the spirit of '76. Actually she was 77, but playing along with her made us all happier."

Lucky day

John Ferrintino and his 4-year-old son, Jonathan, were on their very first fishing trip.

As John was showing the 4-year-old how to put a worm on the hook, Jonathan cut his finger and started to bleed.

"I quickly made up a story to divert his pain," John said. "I told him when a fisherman cuts his finger and draws blood, it gives him good luck. With that, he threw out his line, and, within 30 seconds, Jonathan caught a fish. I silently looked to the sky and knew there was a God.

"Excited by his catch, he quickly put another worm on the hook but ended up cutting another finger. This time, he drew even more blood.

"Through his tears, Jonathan exclaimed, 'Wow, I'm really having a lucky day!'"

Can we talk, dad?

Dan Hurst bought his 16-year-old son, Eric, a car. The first week he drove the car, Eric hit a pothole and shattered a tire. Knowing his son had probably been speeding, Dan felt some sort of punishment was called for.

In his "Father Knows Best" voice, Dan continues the story:

"I thought about grounding him or taking away the car for a period of time. But then I would be forced to take him everywhere, and that would defeat the purpose of the car. I even thought about having him write a 1,000 times, 'I will not speed.'

"I waited until I cooled off before deciding on a punishment. Finally, I told him he would have to take responsibility for his actions and pay the $55 for a new tire. Eric agreed but wanted to ask me one question.

"With the utmost sincerity he asked, 'Dad, do you think I could borrow $55?'

"I couldn't help it; I burst out laughing. Eric didn't understand why I was laughing. That made me laugh even harder. Soon, Eric realized how silly his question was and began to chuckle himself. Then, with both of us laughing, he suggested yard work or household chores to pay off his debt. I readily agreed.

"Our ability to laugh brought us closer and still taught him a valuable lesson in responsibility."

Oh come on, that's funny

Another one of Dan's sons, Jordan, was in a swimming competition. He was one of the best swimmers at the meet and stood a good chance of winning his race.

In the prerace excitement, Jordan stood on the starting platform, still wearing the bottoms of his sweat suit. Everyone was cheering for their favorite swimmers, and Jordan couldn't hear his parents or his coach yelling at him to take off his pants.

The starting gun went off, and Jordan hit the water, still not realizing he was wearing the sweats. He struggled through the race, finishing dead last.

Both parents tried to console Jordan, but he was humiliated. It had nothing to do with finishing last; his embarrassment over diving into the water with his pants on consumed him.

An hour after they got home, Jordan's older brother Jared walked into the house shouting.

"You're not going to believe this," Jared said with a laugh. "Some guy at the meet jumped into the pool without taking off his sweats."

Jordan quickly said, "That's not funny."

"Are you kidding?" Jared shot back. "It's hysterical."

"No it isn't," Jordan insisted.

When his brother asked him why it wasn't funny, Jordan blurted out, "Because it was me."

Jared roared with laughter. "Now, it's definitely funny!" he said. With that, even Jordan began to chuckle.

Magic words … guaranteed

Laughing with our parents cements the family bond. If you don't believe me, Valjean Parker's story about her most special day will convince you.

It was Valjean Parker's wedding day. As she waited at the back of the church, she thought about how emotional her father would be. If it had anything to do with his daughter, Duane Parker could go through a warehouse full of tissues. So, walking Valjean down the aisle, meant it was time to call 1-800-KLEENEX.

I'll let Valjean take the story from here:

"As we walked down the aisle, Daddy started to weep. Fortunately, however, before the wedding I had asked Mom if she had any suggestions to keep Daddy from crying. She told me a story with a magical phrase that always made him laugh.

"I'm glad I was prepared. As we started down the aisle, I turned to him and whispered in Daddy's ear what I had once said as a child, standing outside my parents' bedroom door.

'Quit moving furniture in there. I'm trying to sleep!'

"The look on his face was priceless. Not only did Daddy smile, but he started laughing.

"Walking down the aisle giggling with my father was one of the most special moments of my life."

Chapter 5

You Just
Have to Laugh...
At Yourself

"If I were given the opportunity to present a
gift to the next generation, it would be the
ability for each individual to learn to laugh
at himself."

"Peanuts" creator Charles Schultz

It starts with you. The ability to laugh at yourself
is essential to living life with a **humorous perspective.**

We all do and say things that can be embarrass-
ing. When that happens, some of us get mad and lash
out at others. Some people keep it inside and beat
themselves up emotionally. You don't have to do that.
Laughing when you feel uncomfortable allows you to
Bounce Off the Internal Negative Garbage (BOING).

Another major factor in laughing at yourself is
the ability to find humor in your physical realities.
Sometimes it isn't easy to look in the mirror and
laugh about that receding hairline, expanding waist, or
the serious effects of gravity—but enough about me.

I've met people who have either been born with
handicaps or physical abnormalities, yet these incredible people have discovered laughter is the winning
hand in the cards life has dealt them.

One of these people is Dan Black, who I met
before a comedy show in Lansing, Mich. I sat down to
talk with him specifically for one reason—Dan is a
dwarf, and a comedy routine in my act involved a
dwarf. I wanted to find out from Dan if he would be
offended by this story. He listened, laughed, and said,
"Let's have some fun!"

Here's how I delivered the routine that night:

"It amazes me that people will spend $50,000 for a watch. What gets me is that even though the watch cost you $50,000, you still have to look at the watch to see what time it is. It doesn't tell you what time it is.

"At that price, it should tell you the time. Heck, it should be clairvoyant and know your name. All you should have to do is just think, 'I wonder what time it is?' and that $50,000 baby on your wrist should scream out: 'It's 9:56 p.m., Dave.'

"Who would buy a watch like this? Obviously, somebody who wants to impress their friends. They dream for the day their friends ask what time it is, so they can hold out that watch and say, 'You tell me.'

"Now, if I had 50 grand to blow on telling time, I would impress my friends in another way. I wouldn't buy a watch. I would hire a dwarf, full time, so whenever I wanted to know the time, he would jump out and say, 'It's 8 o'clock. Dave.'"

That night in Lansing, the routine got a good laugh. But then, about 10 minutes later, after I finished another joke, my new friend, Dan, ran on stage and yelled, "It's 9:32, Mr. Naster."

It brought down the house. I don't think I've ever heard an audience erupt like that in all the years I've been performing. All because Dan Black was willing to laugh at himself!

This chapter is filled with stories of people who have been willing to laugh at themselves. Let's continue the "short" story theme.

Altitudinally challenged

Joy Wyler is the director of legal affairs at Children's Mercy Hospital in Kansas City, Mo. She is also a dwarf. She told me about the ridiculous comments people make about her size and how she finds the humor in them.

"A question I get all the time is, 'Have you always been short?'" Joy said. "Sometimes I'll answer with, 'No, the shower was so hot it shrunk me.'"

"People tend to be nervous and uncomfortable when they first notice my size. I use humor and laughter to put them at ease. When I do public speaking, I say, 'I'm not going to use the podium because they haven't finished the elevator in it yet.' Or, I'll say 'Gentlemen, my view of the world is different than yours, so please remove your wallets. It makes your rear look bigger.'

"Some people also talk about me like I'm not there. They'll whisper things like, 'How does she drive or use the facilities?' I'll say something like, 'I'm short, I'm not deaf.'"

Joy is a member of the Little People of America. This group of dwarves holds annual conferences, where they meet and discuss issues related to their size. One year, Joy and her friends were in their hotel and wanted some ice. I'll let Joy continue the story:

"The ice machines were tall, and the ice was deep inside of them. So one of the guys got down on all fours, while another stood on his back and reached in for the ice.

"Now, the guy reaching for the ice was from Texas, and he wore cowboy boots and a huge belt buckle. As he reached in for the ice, he almost fell in. Then, he got stuck when his belt buckle caught on the edge of the ice machine.

"We all laughed so hard we could barely stand up. It kept us laughing for days, thinking of this short-statured cowboy hanging off the ice machine by his belt buckle!

"We're always joking around and laughing about our unique angle on the world."

It's true, the entire time I spoke with Joy Wyler, we were laughing. At her suggestion, I talked to another dwarf, Len Sawisch. He is the director of communications for the state of Michigan's Civil Service Department, and he holds a doctorate degree in psychology.

"You know, I like to use humor, especially when I do public speaking," Len told me. "I'll start off my talk by saying, 'I know what a lot of you might be thinking when you look at me. You are saying to yourself, 'Man, this guy is balding.' Well, maybe if people would quit patting me on the head like I was some little kid, this balding would stop."

Len told me about the time he went camping with a fellow dwarf. Some kids came up to them and asked, "Are you guys midgets?"

"No, it's a costume," was his friend's retort.

"This made us laugh so much we decided to have T-shirts made," said Len. "The front read, 'Real Life

Dwarf' and on the back they said, 'No, it's a costume.' At a Little People of America meeting in Denver we designed T-shirts that read 'Mile High Dwarf' on the front, and on the back 'Altitudinally Challenged'.

"By making and wearing those T-shirts, we kept our sense of humor in spite of some of the demeaning and rude comments that are made to dwarves."

Len's T-shirt buddy was Dan Black, the dwarf who helped me bring down the house so many years before in Lansing, Mich.

With Len's help, I caught up with Dan and found his sense of humor sharper than ever. He told me about going to a fancy restaurant, the kind of place that demanded that men wear jackets. If a man came without one, the restaurant would provide one for him.

Dan didn't have a jacket, so the maître d' brought him one, despite the fact that this jacket would be huge on a dwarf. Dan insisted on wearing this over-sized jacket and laughed all the way through dinner.

If Joy, Len, and Dan can laugh at their altitude, then we can all learn to laugh at our attitude, especially when we make mistakes.

Have a nice day

Paul Hill was a police officer for the state of Colorado. One day, while shooting radar, he clocked a green Jaguar doing 80 miles an hour on Interstate 70 west of Denver. The posted speed limit on this stretch of highway was 55.

I'll let Paul take the story from here:

"I approached the driver's side of the car and asked to see a license and registration. I told the man he was speeding, and he insisted he was not. I explained to him that I had him on the radar gun doing 80, but the man was adamant. He said, 'Officer, I was not driving 80 miles per hour.'

"Trying to control my temper, I leaned into the window to confront the man, when I realized something—this car was an English model with the steering wheel on the right side. I had been talking to the passenger, who indeed had not been driving 80 miles per hour. The driver was on the other side of the car.

"Embarrassed, I told the man, 'Sir, you are correct. You were not driving 80 miles per hour. My mistake. Sorry for the inconvenience and have a nice day.'

"I got back in my patrol car and drove away."

Nap time

This story is from a high school teacher in Kansas. This young woman wished to remain anonymous; once you read the story, you'll understand why.

"It was my first year of teaching, and my most challenging class came in the last hour of the school day. Teaching high school psychology is hard enough, but when the room is filled with members of the varsity football team, your work is cut out for you.

"Early in the school year, the team was going through twice-a-day practice sessions. By the time they got to their last class, these guys were really tired, and there was a lot of sleeping going on in my class.

"Finally, running out of patience with my snoozing students, I lost it. I started yelling. I ended my short tirade by screaming, 'Since all of you like sleeping so much, you all can just sleep with me, after school.'

"I was so mad that I didn't even realize what I'd said. The students got it right away and erupted in laughter. And when my red face gave away the fact that I finally got it, they laughed even louder."

There's no whining in comedy

Laughing at your mistakes is one thing; the ability to find humor in your failings is more difficult. Sometimes we get lucky, and the **TOSS** of a good friend's **humor grenade** helps us find the laughter.

Comic magician John Ferrentino was the opening act for rock 'n' roll legends Crosby, Stills & Nash during several of their national tours.

One time, when the tour stopped in Philadelphia, John invited all of his buddies from New York to come down and watch him work with their rock 'n' roll idols.

The night didn't go as he expected.

John, take it away:

"I was being heckled by the sold-out crowd that wanted to see Crosby, Stills & Nash, not comedy and magic. As the crowd's booing got louder and the comments got more obscene, I began cutting my show.

After using my best material and not drawing any laughs, I knew it was time to go.

"As I walked off the stage with my tail between my legs, I wasn't thinking about my friends who just saw me bomb. I was thinking about getting fired and losing the gig. I was so upset, I was almost crying.

"The first person to greet me was David Crosby. We were always laughing and joking around with each other, but this time, he had a very concerned look on his face.

"David opened up his arms and hugged me. Then, he said, 'Man, they really hated you.'

"I broke our embrace, and he looked even more serious when he said, 'I mean it, they really hated you.' I remember staring at him, wondering how a friend could be so mean.

"That's when he got this big grin on his face and said, 'Nice way to impress your friends, Ferrentino!' I started laughing. It's just what I needed, and David knew it. Once I laughed, I felt better."

Handling life's curveballs will test anyone's **humorous perspective.** It's those who continue to laugh who hit the home runs.

Wanna dance?

Sheila lost one of her legs when her car was hit by a drunk driver. When she realized her leg was gone, Sheila said to herself, "It can't get any worse than this."

That attitude helped her through the aftermath of the accident. Despite wearing a prosthesis, she enjoys many of the activities she participated in before, like playing softball and square dancing. Every Halloween, she has fun with her fake limb, turning it backwards, or dressing it up with different shoes.

One time, Sheila and her girlfriend, Gerry, were at a night club. Also there that evening was a guy who thought he was God's gift to women. He strutted around the club, asking every woman he passed if she wanted to dance. Everyone turned him down because he was drunk and obnoxious.

This guy wouldn't take no for an answer, however, and made another trip through the club. When he finally got to Sheila, she had seen enough. She took off her leg, waved it in his face and snapped "I don't dance. OK?"

The color drained from his face as everyone at the table laughed. Sheila was the last person he asked to dance that night; he left the club, mumbling to himself.

The lung and the sport of it

Stu Swersie has lived his whole life with an active **jester.** He sent me this letter when he heard about this book from his son, Jack:

"I have emphysema. Not just emphysema but EMPHYSEMA. I carefully cultivated this condition one tasty cigarette at a time during a 37-year period. Today, by the way of paying the piper (no pun intended), I'm tethered to an oxygen tank 24 hours a day just to breathe without turning blue.

"I've been told that emphysema is terminal but can take as long as 20 years to reach that stage. Figuring that I could get hit by a bus tomorrow, I'll take that 24 prediction and make the best of it.

"With these semi-debilitating conditions, you find you have lots of time on your hands and comparatively little to do. So it was with great anticipation that I opened the application I received from the E.O.C., the Emphysema Olympic Committee.

"Looking over the application, I saw the usual events listed: the 10-yard underwater relay without oxygen, the 4-inch speed bump jump, the downhill wheelchair slalom, the oxygen tank toss, and the ever-popular balloon blow-ups. Highlighting the games is the exciting metric-mile run, which starts Monday, and, if estimates are correct, will finish late on Wednesday.

"These are exciting times. I can't wait for the games to begin. The thought of it leaves me breathless."

Seize the day

Diana Strudwick is a registered nurse who suffers from a seizure disorder. She explained it to me:

"My seizures don't last long. I just freeze and stare for a few seconds. Others may think I'm just thinking or wandering off, but I'm actually having a seizure.

"One time I was playing blackjack at a casino with a friend, and I went into a seizure. Nobody knew it, including him. I not only won, I won big on an impossible hand. The funny thing was, I missed it all."

The National Epileptic Foundation had a contest to name a newsletter. Diana's suggestion was Seize the Day. "I thought it would be hilarious," said Diana. "Some of my humor is a bit hard for others to take. I have lived with my disorder and have learned to laugh through it. As a nurse, I've learned that you not only have to laugh at yourself, but you have to laugh at the conditions around you.

"For example, I worked at one hospital where a very troubled patient jumped from the roof to his death. Ironically, he landed in front of a sign that reads Patient Drop Off.

"As a nurse, if I don't see the humor around me, I'd go nuts. If I don't appreciate my humorous quali-ties, I may jump one day myself. But knowing me, I'd probably land in front of a sign that read Employee of the Month."

Your knees buckle, but your belt won't

Learning to laugh at yourself leads to a long and happy life. It comes in handy when the hearing goes, the eyesight fails, and your world doesn't spin quite as fast as it used to.

Millie Weintrub introduced herself after one of my **humorous perspective** talks on a cruise ship. She is a senior citizen who loves to tell senior jokes. Millie told me that some seniors get mad at her because they think the jokes are mean. She disagrees.

"I think the jokes are funny," said Millie. "They're just jokes, for goodness sakes. I think the people who get mad are just grumpy, and they've probably never laughed their entire lives."

Millie told me that seniors were the leading carrier of *aids*: hearing *aids*, walking *aids*, medical *aids*, government *aids*, and monetary *aids* to their kids.

Here are some of Millie's favorite lines for the statement: You know you're getting older when...

>   ...Your knees buckle, but your belt won't.
>   ...Everything hurts, and when it doesn't hurt, it doesn't work.
>   ...You know all the answers, but nobody asks the question.
>   ...Dialing long-distance wears you out.
>   ...You sink your teeth into a juicy steak, and they stay there.

Chapter 6

You Just
Have to Laugh…
At Your Job

"People do not quit playing because they
grow old. They grow old because they quit
playing. "

Oliver Wendall Holmes

Thank goodness there are people in the workplace
who have decided to approach their jobs with ready
smiles, hearty laughs, and an arsenal of **humor grenades**.

The pressures of dealing with our duties, our
boss, our clients, and our fellow employees might be
the greatest stress we face every workday. So along
with your briefcase and lunch, don't forget to pack
your **humorous perspective.**

When you find the humor in your job, those
long, boring meetings don't seem so bad. The work
load lightens. You don't spend all day waiting for the
day to end. Sick days? You won't need no stinking sick
days. Vacation? You get a little bit of that every time
you laugh.

Let me introduce you to some people we would
all enjoy working with.

Can you feel the love?

Jeff Frank sat in his cubicle, listening to two fellow employees argue. The discussion became heated,
escalating into a shouting match. Jeff became uncomfortable and found it impossible to work.

When there was a break in the argument, Jeff
stood on his desk, looked out over the top of the cubi-

cles and shouted, "Can you feel the love in the room?"

"Sure, everyone laughed," Jeff said, "but, I did it for myself. That's how I had to ease my own tension. The fact that it helped others was a perk."

Jeff does things like that all the time. He was working at a convention once that was plagued by problems. The catering department wasn't prepared, the hotel ballroom wasn't set up, and the technical equipment hadn't arrived. Jeff walked in to find his client stressed out.

"I knew this man was going to explode," said Jeff. "It was a madhouse in there. I was in there for only five seconds, and I was uncomfortable. What this guy didn't need was somebody like me adding to the chaos.

"So, I went up to him and said, 'Hi, I'm here to help. Would you like me to leave now?'

"For a second, it looked like he was going to punch me. Then he realized what I said and let out a loud laugh.

"I smiled as I walked away laughing."

Whistle while you work

When Tom Murphy became the national sales director of the giant telecommunications company Sprint, he decided to shake things up.

Normally, the national sales meeting was an endless parade of long-winded speakers and conservative executives. The excitement level could only be matched by watching paint dry.

Tom wanted to change that and have some fun at his first meeting. As the sales force waited to meet their new boss, all they saw on stage was a 10-foot cardboard rocket. Then, with rock 'n' roll music blaring through the convention hall, Tom took the stage wearing a space suit. The theme of his comments: Our sales will rocket this year.

If you think that got their attention, the next year he took the stage dressed as Gen. George Patton in full battle gear.

"I can't make everybody laugh, but I can create an atmosphere of being less serious," Tom said. "I don't believe in having just one 'Fun Friday' a month like other companies. I want all the members of my team to enjoy themselves every day. I expect 110 percent out of them, and that's easier to get when they're happy."

Around his office, they have weekly contests for "weirdest" tie and "most creative" earrings.

"One time I started a meeting by saying, 'A lot of you have asked me about some of the new business buzz words, and I'm here to provide explanations,' Tom said. 'First off, mainstream means blow up the organization. Downsize simply means see you later.' They loved it. We all had a good laugh, and then we got down to business.

"We've retained employees in our department because of our humorous work environment. A member of our team was about to transfer to another part of the company, but he decided to stay because of our fun and highly productive atmosphere."

Tom learned the power of humor early in his sales career. When a potential client wouldn't take his calls, Tom took a different approach. He called back, pretending to be a man trying to deliver a load of manure to the client's home. He asked the secretary if he should dump it in the front yard, the back yard, or in the middle of the driveway.

It didn't take long for the client to get on the line himself. That's when Tom explained who he really was.

"After I got the client's business, he told me 'I had to meet you. I figured any guy who is that fearless and creative and made me laugh that hard, I've got to meet,'" Tom said.

"My philosophy is simple. Individual value is not measured on individual success, but how successful you make the people around you. Finding the humor and laughing are key elements in that equation.

"I am also known around the office as the whistler. When my team hears me whistling, things are good. That's why I make sure I whistle all the time."

A quick response

Gavin Klarmann's office in South Africa is much like those in America. The phone is always ringing, and there never seem to be enough bodies around to answer.

"One of my colleagues was particularly notorious for returning calls several days later," Gavin told me. "While he was out of the office, one of his irate clients called. This man was exasperated and complained that he usually had to leave six or seven messages before receiving a return call.

"Sensing his anger, I said, 'Sir, I'll write out a message for him. Then, I'll make five copies of the message and leave all six of them on his desk. That should insure a quick response.'

"As I said goodbye, I could hear him chuckling."

Tickle me Melvin

Melvin Needham works for an insurance agency in Freistatt, Mo. Answering the phone one day, he found an irate woman on the other end. She had just received notice that her insurance policy had been canceled.

Melvin checked the records and discovered the cancellation notice had been mistakenly sent out by the office computer. This explanation did nothing to soothe the woman's anger.

"She continued to give me a good chewing out," Melvin said. "No matter what I said, she got madder and madder. I reminded her it was the computer's fault. She snapped back with, 'Well, maybe you should go give your computer a good cussing,' and slammed down the phone.

"I sat there and thought about what she said. 'Go give that computer a good cussing.' For some reason, that just tickled me, and I started laughing. The more I thought about cussing out that computer, the louder and harder I laughed. I told the ladies in my office what the client had said, and they laughed too.

"You know, I was getting pretty mad talking to that lady. But by laughing at what she said, I got to feeling better."

Breathe normal

The philosopher Voltaire once wrote, "The art of medicine consists of keeping the patient amused while nature heals the disease."

Dr. Gary Baker lives those words. One day he invited me to join him on his rounds, so I could observe his technique.

We scrubbed up, put on hospital gowns, and began his daily routine before surgery. We walked into the room where a woman was waiting for him. Dr. Gary smiled at her and said, "I need to anesthetize your hand before we begin, unless you'd like to skip the formalities and let me just start cutting."

That drew a chuckle, and that little bit of humor seemed to relax her. Dr. Gary pulled out a syringe and said, "I need you to just turn your head the other way while I begin to anesthetize you. I want you to continue to breathe normally—or you could hold your breath, turn blue, pass out, and then we'll have to start all over again."

The woman started laughing and didn't even notice the needle when it went into her skin.

We walked into another room, and Dr. Gary said, "I'm so excited! This is the first time I've done this operation without the procedure book." Everybody laughed, including the patient.

"It's a win-win situation," said Dr. Gary in explaining his philosophy. "I like to make people laugh. It puts me in a great mood to operate, and my patients are in a better frame of mind to be operated on. Believe me, if both of us are relaxed, it's better for everyone."

Learn to laugh

Deb Anthony is a hospice nurse. She works under some of the most difficult conditions facing anyone in the medical profession. No matter what Deb does, her patients are going to die.

So where do humor and laughter come in? When Deb learned about this book, she wrote me this letter. I'd like to share her words with you:

"Hospice humor? You've got to be kidding! What could you laugh at in a hospice? Death and dying? Grief? That's serious stuff. But you learn. You learn to laugh.

"You laugh with the patient who took the teddy bear you brought him, found it a mate, and on your next visit, showed you his proud family of three baby bears.

"You laugh at yourself when you assume that the loving, attentive person at the patient's bedside is her husband, only to find out he's her son-in-law.

"You laugh with a co-worker who missed the meeting where you discussed the patient who shot mice in his home with his rifle, only to see his marksmanship, first hand, unsuspectingly that week.

"You laugh at the teaching session to show the staff the procedure for changing the rolls of toilet paper. You laugh when the nurse who kept complaining about a foul odor later found a dead mouse in her pocket.

"You learn to look for humor and create it in your life, to ease stress. You learn laughter can relieve pain with an effect similar to medications, and with far fewer side effects.

"You learn to take what you do serious but take what you are lightly. You learn laughter adds life to the days of a dying patient and to the lives of those who love them.

"You learn the most deadly of all life-threatening conditions is not cancer, heart disease, or even AIDS. It is the absence of laughter. It causes more suffering than any disease, and no amount of medicine can relieve it's pain.

"And yet, it is easily curable, simply by learning to laugh."

Dumb questions

The S.S. Norway is the largest cruise ship in the Norwegian Cruise Lines fleet. When the boat is full, as it usually is, there are more than 2,200 passengers on board for the week-long cruises.

The folks who work in the gift shops on these ships have to deal with requests and questions that sometimes border on the unbelievable. While it would be bad business to laugh at the passengers, the staff does have some fun by keeping a record of the ridiculous comments. Then, after work, they head for the crew bar to have a laugh.

Charley Hilton, a sales clerk told me, "If we didn't have a good laugh, we'd be tempted to throw some of the passengers overboard."

Here are some examples from the staff's list:

Customer: Where is the gift shop?
Clerk: Which one, sir? We have nine of them.
Customer: Oh, I don't know, any of them.
Clerk: Well, sir, you are standing in one, now.
Customer: No, the one with the watches.

A passenger asked a gift shop clerk who was standing in front of an elevator, "Excuse me, does this elevator go to the front of the ship?"

Standing at the jewelry counter a man asked, "Why is this diamond shining red?"
The clerk answered, "Because, sir, it's a ruby."

A table covered with watches featured a large sign which read "All Watches $69.95." A woman pointed to a watch and asked the sales clerk, "So how much is this watch?"

The clerk said, "All the watches on this table are $69.95." The passenger picked up another watch and asked, "So how much is this one?"

"How much are these T-shirts?" asked a passenger. The sales clerk asked which ones he was referring to. The passenger said, "The ones for $9.95."

There are some people who believe there are no dumb questions, just dumb answers. Those people never worked retail. Think about your place of employment. I bet you can put together your own list of dumb questions from clients, customers, even fellow employees. Do it, and enjoy the laughs.

Thanks, mom

Several years ago, Wayne C. Chappell worked in Baltimore as president of the convention and visitors bureau. Part of his job was scheduling conventions and meetings at various venues throughout the city.

One year, Wayne had to move the annual Baltimore Flower Show out of its long-time location because a far more lucrative convention wanted the meeting space. Wayne tells the following story:

"Within an hour of my decision on the Flower Show, I received a call from the office of Mayor William Donald Schaefer and was ordered to his office immediately. By the time I arrived, the Mayor's conference room was crowded with people from the Flower

Society and other interested parties who wanted to keep the Flower Show at the convention center.

"As I looked around the room, I realized these were either the most important people in Baltimore, or the wives of the most influential citizens. The mayor obviously had votes in mind.

"A lovely elderly woman began the meeting with a plea for the Flower Show, and she explained why it was so important to the city. As she concluded her emotional talk, the room filled with applause.

"Then it was my turn. I bolstered myself up by reminding myself that I had all my arguments ready to go. The fact that I was so outnumbered shouldn't bother me, I reasoned. I knew making this change was the right thing to do. I felt the mayor would eventually agree with me.

"As the applause for the elderly woman ended, mayor Schaefer stood and said, 'Thank you, Mother.' The mayor looked at me and smiled. It really was his mother. The mayor shrugged his shoulders and began laughing. I laughed, too; then everyone in the room broke up.

"The laughter released all the tension, and we were able to reach an agreement for another, even better location for the annual Flower Show."

I dozed off

Jim Teeter is a comedian. Like many of us in the comedy business, he had to hold other jobs to make ends meet during the struggling early years.

"I was waiting for more than an hour in this office lobby for a job interview," Jim said. "I ended up falling asleep. I woke up when the man who was about to interview me said, 'I wish I could take a nap in the afternoon.'

"With a grin on my face I said, 'You could, if you were interviewing for a job in this place.' He laughed and apologized for keeping me waiting. I ended up getting the job."

That's t-u-t-u

"When I laugh, it makes the day more fun."

That's the first comment I heard from Jerry Bressel, a lawyer who specializes in divorce cases. "Dissolving a marriage is never an easy thing," said Jerry. "Keeping a **humorous perspective** is one way to deal with stress, emotional clients, and fellow lawyers, no matter what kind of case.

"We give every one of our cases themes, and some even have their own theme songs. One time we were in a panic because we had not come up with a theme for a particular case, which involved a dog named Nasty who had bitten someone. We began singing the song 'Nasty Girl' by Janet Jackson, and then we started dancing around outside the courtroom.

"The judge's administrative assistant came around the corner just in time to see our little routine. She burst out laughing and later told us we had made her bad day a better one.

"In one case I tried, the jury liked our sense of humor so much they interrupted the judge one morning asking, 'Isn't Mr. Bressel going to be here today?' They even asked the judge if they could give our client some money, even though he was the one being sued. The fact the jury wanted to give us money was a first, and I know it was because of our humor.

"In another divorce case, we represented the husband. There was a mistake made when the separation agreement was typed up, and it read as if the husband wanted all of his wife's clothing.

"The wife's lawyer jumped up and accused the husband of being a cross-dresser, mocking his desire for her clothing. I immediately piped in and said, 'Excuse me your honor, we also want all of the accessories that go with those clothes.'

"Everybody including the judge burst out laughing. It made the other lawyer look ridiculous."

Jerry doesn't restrict his humor to the courtroom. While I visited with him in his office, he picked up the phone and called a lawyer at another firm. When the operator informed him that the lawyer was unavailable, Jerry's **jester** kicked in.

"Please tell John that we had to let out the waistband on his tutu for the dance recital," Jerry said. "That's t-u-t-u. I also need to know if he wants the sparkles or wants to just leave it white. I think the sparkles will work better with his complexion. Have you got that?"

I heard her repeat over the speaker phone, "That's t-u-t-u." As she spelled it out, I had to cover my mouth to keep from laughing out loud.

"You see, David, that message will be all over his office in an hour, and he'll call back and we'll have a good laugh," said Jerry. "That's how I deal with tension and stress."

If it pleases the court

Just as the cruise ship staff collected dumb questions, a lawyer friend of mine collects incredibly ridiculous excerpts from actual courtroom proceedings. Here are some samples:

Q: When was the last time you saw Michael?
A: At his funeral.
Q: Did he make any comments to you at that time?

Q: Doctor, as a result of your examination of the plaintiff, is the young lady pregnant?
A: The young lady is pregnant—but not as a result of my examination.

Q: Any suggestions as to what prevented this from being a murder trial instead of an attempted murder trial?
A: The victim lived.

Q: I'll show you exhibit three and ask you if you recognize that picture?

A: That's me.

Q: Were you present at the time the picture was taken?

Q: What happened then?

A: He told me "I'll have to kill you because you can identify me."

Q: Did he kill you?

Q: Doctor, before you performed the autopsy, did you check for a pulse?

A: No.

Q: Did you check for blood pressure?

A: No.

Q: Did you check for breathing?

A: No.

Q: So, then it is possible that the patient was alive when you began the autopsy?

A: No.

Q: How can you be so sure, doctor?

A: Because his brain was sitting on my desk in a jar.

Q: But could the patient have still been alive nevertheless?

A: It is possible that he could have been alive and practicing law somewhere.

Call 9-1-1

If you ever go to Miami, you must stop and see SAMY, hairdresser to the stars.

His salon is in the swank Radisson Hotel on 72nd Avenue, and his clients include singer Gloria Estefan, former First Lady Barbara Bush, and anybody who is anybody in the Miami area. SAMY's line of beauty products is distributed worldwide.

He radiates a well-coifed **humorous perspective,** which SAMY told me is a very important part of his job. Here's what he says:

"I have to be careful not to laugh or judge my clients, but sometimes a hint of humor is the perfect beauty touch. A woman came into my salon for a scheduled appointment but insisted that I not touch her hair, cut it, or shampoo it. Despite her comments, I went ahead and started on her hair.

"She continued to whine and complain loudly, saying, 'If you touch my hair, I'll die. If you cut my hair, I'll die.'

"The entire salon became uncomfortably silent. Loud enough for everyone to hear, I said, 'Someone call 9-1-1. Get an ambulance. Call a medic or the coroner because I am about to work on this lady's hair and make her gorgeous.'

"You could hear a bobby pin drop. I think I actually heard one. When I saw a brief smile on the woman's face, I continued to work as if nothing had happened.

"I love it when I make someone look good, but when I make them feel good, I have a customer for life."

Finally, I'm on solid ground

I was working on a cruise ship that was anchored off an island in the Bahamas. Smaller tender boats were used to shuttle passengers from the ship to this tropical paradise.

On this particular day, the weather was bad and got progressively worse. A strong wind and high waves made the tender ride pretty bumpy. At one point, the conditions were so bad the captain had to reposition the cruise ship while the passengers returning to the ship on the tender boats sat in a bumpy holding pattern, which lasted for more than an hour.

By the time the tenders were able to pull alongside the ship, all the passengers were drenched. A few were still in a festive mood (thanks to the rum), some were seasick (thanks to the rum), others were annoyed (not enough rum), while some were downright scared.

I was assisting people back onto the ship when I saw one lady stumble across the gangway. As her first foot landed on the ship, she said, "Finally, I'm on solid ground." With that, she fainted.

Paul Hill was on duty that day. He is a diving instructor and a member of the ship's Special Emergency Response Team. Paul assisted her immediately, and she came to within seconds.

As she opened her eyes, Paul said to her, "Ma'am, you passed out, but you're OK now. We're going to take you up to the infirmary, but we don't want you to walk, so we're going to move you to this stretcher. Now the man helping me here is a firefighter, just in case you burst into flames during the move."

In her confused state, it took several seconds for her to realize what Paul said. As they carried her off on the stretcher, I heard her laugh. Her fear and tension were distracted, thanks to Paul's perfectly TOSSed **humor grenade.**

He loves to fly

Captain Robert C. Lucek is a pilot for United Airlines. During the years, he told me how pilots have found humor in the friendly skies. Here are some of his stories:

"An airline was experimenting with a camera in the cockpit so the passengers could actually watch the pilots fly the plane. The thinking was that by watching the pilots in action, the passengers would feel safer and learn more about just what pilots do in the cockpit.

"One day the pilots used a gorilla's arm to show the passengers how this worked. At one point during the flight, they handed this gorilla's arm a banana. The guys in the cockpit thought it was hysterical and thought the passengers would love it. They were wrong. Most of the passengers didn't appreciate their monkeying around and complained to the airline.

"Another pilot would blow a train whistle over the plane's PA system just as they were pulling away from the gate.

"I laugh every time I remember one of my co-pilots who was explaining the Great Salt Lake as we were flying over Utah. He talked about the 'microorgasms' in the water instead of 'microorganisms.' We could hear the passengers laughing all the way up front.

"It's the everyday stuff that cracks me up. I just love to laugh."

She loves to fly

In today's world, most of us get on and off airplanes so often we don't think about the process anymore. We tune out the flight attendants and their pretakeoff announcement about seat backs and tray tables, forgetting this speech is done for our safety.

A flight attendant for Southwest Airlines, who chooses to be called Joanne, uses humor to regain the attention of frequent fliers. Here's what I heard Joanne say on a recent Southwest flight:

"Ladies and gentlemen, if you could please give your attention to the other flight attendants, who include my husband, Dave, and his ex-wife, Susan, they'd like to point out the safety features of the aircraft. For those of you who haven't been in an automobile lately and used your seat belt, slide the flat end into the buckle. To release, lift up on the flip-latch and it will separate. Tying the belts together is not acceptable.

"I know they've told you there are 50 ways to leave your lover. Unfortunately, we have only six ways on this aircraft: two forward entry doors, two over the wing exits, and two back exit doors. All are clearly marked with red exit signs and the disco lighting along the aisle will lead you to them.

"In the seat back pocket in front of you, or to the side if you are sitting in one of our 'plush' lounge areas, you should find an emergency briefing card that further supplements this information on our safety features. Of course, there's no telling what you'll find in those pockets—gum wrappers, candy wrappers, empty cups or cans—and if you dig deep enough, possibly a dirty diaper.

"Since we will be flying over pools, puddles, and hot tubs on our way to Albuquerque today, you'll note your bottom seat cushion may be used as a flotation device in the event of a water evacuation.

"Flight attendants are now walking through the cabin, checking to make sure seat belts are fastened, tray tables are up and locked, that seats are in the forward and most uncomfortable position, and that the carry-on luggage you wished you had checked, is crammed all the way up under the seat in front of you.

"We certainly don't anticipate a change in the cabin pressure, but should one occur, four margarine cups will magically appear overhead. When they do, stop screaming, place the cup over your nose and mouth, and breathe normally until notified by crew members, or until Susan comes by offering mouth-to-mouth. In that case, preferential treatment will be given to those gentlemen with Rolex watches.

"There's no smoking at all on board this aircraft. We prohibit smoking in the lavatories and if we find you doing so, Dave will ask you to step out on the wing, where you can also enjoy our patio furniture and the movie 'Gone With the Wind.'

"Now that we have all of the rules and regulations out of the way, sit back, relax, and enjoy your hour flight. If there's anything else you need during this flight, just forget about it! Just kidding. Don't hesitate to call on Dave. Susan and I will be in the back, finishing our nails."

Joanne had plenty to say when the plane landed as well:

"On behalf of Southwest Airlines and this flight crew, we'd like to be the first to welcome you to Albuquerque. Do us one last favor—keep your tush to the cush, your seat belt fastened, and the luggage right were it is until Captain America and Boy Wonder pull this aircraft up to the gate and turn off the fasten seat belt signs. That will be your only indication that it's safe to jump up, grab all of your luggage, and go absolutely nowhere.

"Thanks for choosing Southwest today. Go out, have a great week, and do come back and see us again, because no one loves your money more than us. Oh, one more note. We have a special gentlemen on board today celebrating his 98th birthday and his first flight. (Everyone on the plane began to applaud.) Do me a big favor and wish our captain a happy birthday on your way out and let him know he doesn't look a day older than 50 (moans and groans from the passengers). I can't believe you all fell for that."

It was fun to hear all the passengers laughing, and they gave Joanne quite an ovation as the plane pulled up to the gate. She told me that people thank her all of time for making them laugh.

Did I tell you it was hot?

I've met many wonderful people throughout the years who saw the world from behind a smile. One of those is Denny Dey. He truly understands the **humorous perspective** He told me this story, and I trust you will hang on his every word.

"It was hot! The temperature was 105 in the shade and the humidity level was a dirty word. It was the kind of heat that turns your own sweat against you. I was a service technician for an air conditioning company and business was good. I was working 'on call' this particular weekend, and company rates normally jumped to $35 per hour, no matter what the problem was.

"I took a call and was sent to a two-story house owned by a couple who had just returned from vacation and found their air conditioner didn't work. They were waiting on me to make life better.

"It was about 4 o'clock in the afternoon when I

got there. I found myself working on the west side of this big white house in full view of the blinding sun. Sweat was racing out of my pores like rats deserting a sinking ship. Sweat was streaming down my arms and hands, and I couldn't hold the tools or the wires. I needed at least two more hands, but there was no one else I could call.

"Just then, the lady of the house stepped onto the back deck right above my head and asked if she could help. I wasn't supposed to let anyone near the work because they might get fried—and that would irritate my boss. But this time, I had no choice. I accepted her dry hands and eager attitude.

"Five minutes later, she had both her hands inside the service box holding important loose ends. I had my arms wound around her arms, tools working furiously. We were cheek to cheek, and I don't mean maybe! We were trading sweat like teenage lovers in the back seat of a car. If somebody had come upon us, I wasn't sure what they would think.

"Well, as I was turning the last screw, her husband walked out on the deck and looked down at the scene. I saw the expression on his face. Needless to say, I was about as intimate as one man can get with another man's wife without the topic of birth control coming up.

"I looked back at the service box, pretending that I wasn't terrified. I whispered just loud enough so that the nice lady could hear me, 'Is this going to be a problem?'

"She didn't miss a beat. She curled her lip up and

blew the sweat away from her eyes and said, 'It's all right. He's a missionary.'

"We all laughed. The air conditioner was promptly fixed, thanks to this woman's cool head and **humorous perspective**."

You won't eat lunch in this class again

Our schools can be fertile grounds for the cultivation of humor. Sometimes, the quickest way to children's minds is through their funny bones. Suggested supplies: a **fun house mirror** and a sackful of **humor grenades**.

Suzanne Sybert is a school teacher, working mostly with eighth graders. She used the **fun house mirror** when her lesson plan was interrupted.

I'll let Suzanne tell you what happened:

"I had a very precocious student who liked to sneak bites of his lunch during class. Every time I turned around to face the blackboard, I could hear the crackling of his lunch sack. When I asked him if he was eating something, he said, 'Of course not.'

"I could see he had something in his mouth while he was answering me, so I decided to have some fun. I had him bring his lunch sack to the front of the room and place it on my desk. When I asked him what was in the sack, he said nothing.

"I said to him, 'Oh you're telling me there isn't a cupcake, or sandwich, or even potato chips in this sack.

As I mentioned each item, I hit the bag, pounding it flat.

"The other students rolled with laughter. The young man didn't laugh, but he never ate his lunch in my classroom again."

Teacher's rule

Rags Smith is a high school teacher in Arkansas City, Kan. She has learned that humor is one of the best teaching tools. I'll let Rags explain herself:

"I carry a tube of very red lipstick, and when students falls asleep in class, I apply it and give them a big kiss on the cheek. After the first few kids left my class with lipstick all over their cheeks, everyone had a good laugh, but they also got the message. Now, I only have to do it a couple times each year. When a student does fall asleep, I go for my makeup bag, and the other students warn him that I am puckering up.

"When a student forgets pencil, paper, etc., and asks to borrow from me, I make them say, 'Please dearest Ms. Rags, whom I love best of all.' The class gets such a kick out of it. They usually remember their supplies the next day. If I forget, the rest of the class instructs the student what to say.

"If a kid gets into the habit of staring at me and trying to make me uncomfortable. I'll just say, 'Oh look. He can't take his eyes off my stunning beauty.' He laughs and stops staring.

"I would go crazy without my laughs, and I'll take them whenever I can find them."

Please execute

Christina Foster is a high school guidance counselor. During the years, she has collected excuses parents have written to explain their children's absence or tardiness. Laughing at the most ridiculous explanations is one of the ways she retains her sanity.

Here are some of those excuses:

- "Please ackuse John been absent of January 28, 29, 30, 22 and 33. John has been absent from school because he had two teeth taken out of his face."
- "Please excuse Gloria. She had been sick and under the doctor."
- "My son is under the doctor's care and should not take P. E. class, please execute."
- "Please excuse Joe Friday. He has loose vowels."
- "Please excuse Blanch from P.E. for a few days. She fell out of a tree and misplaced her hip."
- "Please excuse Joyce from Jim. She is administrating."
- "Please excuse Diane from being absent yesterday. She is in bed with gramps."

Chapter 7

You Just Have to Laugh... At Your Job

(Part 2: Public Service)

Police officers and firefighters constantly deal with the uglier and more gruesome side of life. To protect and serve means they'll put their life on line when needed. Humor and laughing help them deal with that stress and the emotional wounds they collect.

You may recognize Dr. Al Somodevilla from the chapter on laughing with your family.

Doctor Al has a Ph.D. in clinical psychology and has worked both as a consultant and as the chief psychologist for the Dallas Police Department. He now has his own private practice dedicated to helping police and paramedics.

One of Doctor Al's first experiences with policemen and humor came when an officer on the Dallas force committed suicide.

This policeman had recently lost his wife, and from there his life had gone downhill. Unable to deal with his personal problems and the stress of the job, he ended his life by shooting himself in the head.

Doctor Al and two officers were the first on the gruesome scene. After a few minutes, Doctor Al heard the other men laughing. They called to him from the other room, and it wasn't long before Doctor Al was laughing as well.

When the officer shot himself, one of his eyeballs flew out and landed on a portrait hanging on the wall. They made jokes about the cyclops picture and continued to laugh as they investigated the shooting.

The humor helped carry them through what had to be done. But after their work was completed and they left the scene, Doctor Al was with them when they pulled over along a dirt road and one of the officers vomited while the other broke down and cried.

Doctor Al was also on scene after an airplane crash at the Dallas-Fort Worth Airport. He remembers how some of the policemen referred to the burned corpses as "crispy critters" and laughed about which one they should start putting in the body bags, the "white meat or the dark meat."

"They may have been joking and laughing, but I saw the tears rolling down their eyes," said Doctor Al. "That's how they dealt with the morbid reality."

When Doctor Al talks to police departments and academies, he often uses humor. He frequently shows a video that was taken by a camera mounted in the car of a highway patrolman who had just pulled over a woman for speeding. The footage shows her getting out of the car, swearing at the officer, and kicking the patrol car. The officer put his face in front of the camera and said, "Another calm day at the office."

"I explain to the officers that laughing will get many of those bad feelings out of them," Doctor Al said. "If they take it home, they eventually won't have a home. Not many people want to hear the gloom and horror they witness, so they have to get that out some other way. Laughing does just that.

"One officer told me he relaxes by going skiing once a year," Doctor Al recalled. "I asked him what he did the other 51 weeks. If you are laughing every day, 365 days a year, 52 weeks a year, then you're dealing with it. Even though it hurts, you've got to keep laughing."

Doctor Al's words reminded me of John Douglas. He's a former member of the FBI Serial Crime Unit, who wrote the book *The Mind Hunter.* He was one of the first people in the country to come up with the idea that clues from the crime scene could help profile serial killers. He wrote this in his book:

"When you spend your time looking at murder scenes and dump sites—especially those involving children—when you've talked to thousands of victims and their families, when you've seen the absolutely incredible things human beings are capable of doing to other human beings, you'd better be able to laugh."

I hope these comments from Doctor Al and John Douglas help explain many of the stories you are about to read. The comments by some of the policeman and firefighters in these stories might be considered crude or inappropriate. However, by understanding the stress they work under, it is actually miraculous to see how they deal with these challenging situations by laughing. To me, they are our true heroes.

If we're not laughing, we're puking or crying

How do you handle your emotions when your job includes things like finding a man with his head smashed as thin as a writing tablet? Or a child impaled on a fence, with his jacket still hanging above him in the trees?

Ray Lynn, Scott Rolled, and Joe Klebstone are firefighters in Kansas City, Mo. One day, I sat down with them while they waited for the next alarm. They explained to me how they deal with these kind of daily tragedies that are as common for them as coffee breaks are for other people.

"We're either laughing, puking, or crying," Ray said. "And since this is the profession I have chosen, I'm going to laugh."

One time they discovered a dead man laying on the floor, wearing only hiking boots. His body was covered with tattoos and he was holding a single meatball.

"Come on, you have to laugh when you find something like that," said Scott. "Or, when you find someone faking an injury and you see one of the paramedics tying his shoestrings together. You know as soon as he starts walking, he'll fall over."

As we laughed over their stories, an alarm went off. They stopped in mid-yuk and moved immediately toward the fire trucks. The alarm ended up being for another part of the city, so they didn't have to respond, but I was amazed how quickly they shifted emotional gears.

"We're all business when it comes to our job," said Joe. "But we have to laugh at what we see, or we'd be basket cases."

Walk this way

Three firefighters in full gear went racing up a flight of stairs in response to an emergency call. When they arrived at the door, an elderly woman demanded to see identification. One of the firefighters told her to look out her window at the fire truck parked outside. She let them in, and then slammed and locked the door. "OK, I saw the truck," she said, "now I have to tell you..."

The firefighters interrupted her and asked where the fire was. She responded, "Oh, there's no fire. My kitty is stuck in the attic." They asked the woman how to get to the attic. "Walk this way," she said, shuffling along with a stiff gait.

All three firefighters followed behind her, imitating her walk. She couldn't see them, and it was all they could do to keep from screaming out in laughter. It was right out of a Mel Brooks movie.

Here kitty, kitty

A sheriff's office in Colorado received a call about a cat that was trapped somewhere in a house. When the deputies arrived at the scene, they were greeted by a concerned woman who described the cries of the distressed cat.

She guided the deputies to the spot where the sound was apparently coming from. The officers found a wall with no apparent openings, so they were stumped on how to get to the cat. The woman said the deputies could tear into the walls and floorboards and even signed a release absolving them from responsibility for any damages.

They tore into the walls but didn't find anything. They tore into the floor boards. No cat. They tore into other places. No cat.

Finally, the deputies figured out where the sound of the cat was coming from: the screen saver on the family's computer featured a loud "meowing" cat as a reminder that the computer was still turned on.

"We never even thought to ask her if she even owned a cat," said the deputy. "We just assumed she did."

Man, you have to laugh at this stuff.

Free breast exams

Firefighters spend a great deal of time on their shifts waiting. With the stress and tension that goes with their job, these idle moments allow their **humorous perspective** to take over.

"We'll move a guy's car sideways in the bay," one fireman told me. "We'll also pick up a guy who is sleeping, bed and all, and put him outside on the front lawn if he is snoring.

"Our firehouse was right next to a police station. Sometimes we would spray police officers' personal cars with water right before the temperature dropped to twenty degrees—just seeing their faces or hearing them yell when they realized their cars were frozen would draw huge laughs from the guys."

There's a firehouse in Kansas City that sits directly across the street from a gas station. The filling station manager always complained about firefighters parking their cars in front of his lot.

"We called this guy and convinced him we were from a radio station," said a firefighter. "We told him he could win a contest if he followed our instructions. By the end of the conversation, we had this guy hopping up and down on one foot singing 'Here comes Peter Cotton Tail, hopping down the bunny trail.'

"We laughed so hard, we had to run out and tell the guy, because we couldn't take it anymore.

"One guy put out a sign on the front lawn of the station that read Free Breast Exams," a fireman told me. "One woman actually came in for the exam. The guys sent her to the captain who had no idea what she was talking about. The woman finally dragged him outside to see the sign.

"Man we still lose it laughing about that one."

Quit shooting the bull

Detective Ian Millman is a policeman in Vancouver, Canada. He approaches his job with a great deal of dedication and a **humorous perspective**. One of his fellow police officers told me this story.

"A guy was driving a truck through a city park. He was pulling a small trailer that held a couple of bulls. There was an accident, and somehow one of the bulls escaped and started running around the park.

"Before long, there were people all over the park trying to catch this bull. The park turned into a frenzy of activity with tourists scattering everywhere.

"Ian finally cornered the bull. As the frightened animal turned and headed in his direction, he pulled out his gun and shot it several times.

"A photographer for the local paper showed up and asked Ian to pose with one foot on the bull, his hat back, blowing smoke off his gun. Ian did this only after the photographer assured him the picture would not appear in the paper.

"Wrong. The next day it was the lead story, with a picture front and center of Millman standing over the bull. The chief called him in and was fuming. He screamed, 'Look at all of these letters and messages. Do you realize the commotion and problems you have caused me. Do me a favor. Take any single letter out and read it, any letter you like and look at the disturbance you've caused.'

"Ian reached into the stack of letters and pulled one out and read it aloud. It said, in part, that it was nice to see a Vancouver police officer with a sense of humor. Ian started laughing. The chief read the letter and started laughing.

"Both of them end up laughing hysterically, and Millman did not get punished. In fact, he was later promoted."

Within the same Vancouver precinct, there is a bridge where suicidal people think they are going to plummet to their deaths. Unfortunately, or fortunately, depending how you look at it, the fall from the bridge isn't enough to kill anyone.

One time an officer tried valiantly to stop someone from jumping, but the man jumped anyway. The rescue team was already below, and the man was pulled out of the water uninjured.

One of the cops wrote "5.0" and ''5.5" on pieces of paper and held them up for his fellow officers to see, in obvious imitation of Olympic judges holding up scorecards in diving events. All the policemen on the scene got a great laugh out of his antic. But a woman watching the rescue became irate, questioning the officers' actions.

Mr. Scorecard convinced her that he wasn't mocking the situation. Rather, he explained this was how the officers ordered coffee from a distance. "5.0" meant black, "5.5" was for cream and sugar. The woman bought his story and left.

Caution, school zone

Jonathan Beaver is a police officer in St. Joseph, Mo. One day, while shooting radar, he clocked a car doing 70 miles per hour in a school zone.

"I pulled the car over," said Jonathan. "I was so mad, I was shaking. This was during the school day, and this car was 50 miles over the limit. I wanted to reach into the car and shake the driver.

"Barely containing my temper, I told the teenager at the wheel that I had been waiting to catch someone like him all day.

"Without batting an eye, he looked up and said, 'Sir, I got here as fast as I could.'

"I couldn't help but laugh. It definitely cooled me off, but he still got a very expensive ticket."

You should be catching criminals

An Irvine, Texas, police officer pulled a woman over for speeding. She kept insisting that rather than trapping speeders, he should be out catching criminals. She kept asking him if he had some sort of quota he had to reach each day.

Finally, the officer said, "Yes, ma'am, with this ticket I'm giving you, I get a toaster."

She didn't laugh. As a matter of fact, it turned out she was the wife of a high-ranking city official. Her complaints to his superiors led to a reprimand, and he was moved to a more difficult shift.

But a week later, the officer received a letter from the city official, praising his sense of humor and encouraging him to continue using it in public. He also apologized for his wife's failure to see the officer's humor.

The graveyard shift

In Bay City, Mich., a woman was working the midnight shift at a convenience store. When a man entered the store and wandered around for more than 30 minutes, the clerk became frightened he might rob her.

Her adrenaline was pumping when the man approached the checkout counter and presented a can of pork and beans. Relieved, she turned around to ring up the sale on her cash register. When she turned back, she was shocked to see he had exposed himself, placing "it" on the counter.

She immediately picked up the can of pork and beans and slammed it on his exposed part. He passed out and hit the floor. She promptly dialed 9-1-1. The operator told her to get outside and lock the store. She followed instructions and the police arrived within minutes, arresting the man once he regained consciousness.

As the man was escorted out of the store, one of the police officers turned to him and said, "I bet you wish you would've tried to steal a loaf of bread."

Chapter 8

You Just
Have to Laugh...
At Death

.

"See, I told you I was sick!"

Epitaph on a gravestone

There is one constant in life, and that is death. I think there should be another—laughter. This chapter is filled with stories of people who faced life's final chapter with smiles on their faces and a **humorous perspective** They battled physical, emotional, and psychological pain with the most powerful medication on the face of the earth.

Their laughter allowed them to delay and, in some cases, even postpone death. It made a troubled time easier to bear for themselves and their loved ones. Others used humor where death hung in the air like a fog. They laughed in the face of dehumanizing torture because it was the only thing that made them feel better.

Early in my comedy career, I learned about the healing power of laughter. I worked as a mime and clown, performing at elementary schools throughout the world, more than 500 schools in all. The one stop that taught me the most was in the oncology ward at the Kansas University Medical Center.

I was escorted into a room where a dozen children waited for me. All of them were bald. They were either going through chemotherapy or were being prepared for cancer surgery.

Of all the audiences I've appeared in front of, none intimidated me like this group of kids. I was stunned. I thought to myself, "How can I make these kids laugh when they're sick, even dying?"

I shared my concerns with one of the nurses I knew, and she told me to treat these kids like I would any normal, healthy children. So that's what I did. I forgot about the bald heads, the IV tubes attached to their arms, and the pain that sometimes showed on their faces.

The show I did that afternoon turned into one of the best shows of my career. These children were so full of life and laughter that someone listening outside would not have known these were sick children.

I connected with one child in particular. I had a couple of kazoos, and we went up and down the halls of the oncology ward pretending we were motorcycle riders in a race against each other. Kids lined the halls laughing and encouraging us as we ran around making noise like we were riding big Harleys. When the little guy beat me in the race, the hall erupted with cheers and laughter.

This snapshot of life is an image frozen in my mind. Kids were in wheelchairs and hospital beds, but they were having the time of their lives. For the briefest of moments, their laughter controlled their pain.

I don't know how many of those young people are still with us, but I do believe their chances of survival were improved dramatically by their ability to have fun.

Laughter can also help us continue with our lives when loved ones pass away. Recently, I went to the funeral of a friend's father. I did not know Bill Long, but his son, Rob, told me his dad used to listen to me on the radio and was a big comedy fan. According to everything I heard at his eulogy, Bill Long had a grand sense of humor. Friend after friend got up to speak fondly of him, but the story that made everyone smile was told by Bill's brother:

"As children, Bill and I used to get into trouble. One time, Mom ordered us to go out and get a switch. For you youngsters, a switch is a thin branch with some snap to it used for the purpose of spanking unruly children.

"I went out and returned with what Mom ordered, but Bill came back dragging a 3-inch-thick, 3-foot-long tree limb—basically a log. When Mom saw Bill's 'switch,' she started laughing so hard she forgot what she was mad about."

At this point, the funeral service was filled with laughter; it felt as if pure, cool oxygen had been pumped into the room. You could almost see the healing begin. Just as he disarmed his mother with a big branch instead of a switch, Bill Long's humor continued to help people at his own funeral.

Holocaust humor

It seems impossible—laughter in the concentration camps of Nazi Germany? Millions of people died in the Holocaust, brutally murdered in one fashion or another because of their nationality, religion, profession, or sexual orientation.

But history shows us that in this most horrific time, laughter was an escape from the specter of death.

Sylvia Rothchild wrote in *Voices From the Holocaust* about Rachella Velt Meekcoms, a Dutch Jew, who would stage vaudeville shows in the Auschwitz concentration camp with other teen-age inmates.

"In spite of all of our agony and pain, we never lost our ability to laugh at ourselves and our miserable situation," Rachella said, "We had to make jokes to save ourselves from deep depression. We mimicked top overseers, and I did impersonations about the camp life. Somebody did a little tap dance, and others did different funny and crazy things.

"The overseers slipped into the barracks while we weren't looking, and instead of giving us a punishment, they laughed their heads off. I couldn't believe it. One day they were hitting us black and blue, and then they were laughing while we made fun of them."

Rachella survived Auschwitz.

Wigged out

Jaymie Smith was diagnosed with cancer. It was not just one kind of cancer, but two—lymphatic and breast cancer. She went through nine months of chemotherapy and six months of radiation treatments that left her extremely sick and very weak.

Since all of her hair had fallen out from her treatments, she comforted herself with a couple of nice wigs. Once she regained her strength, she began to drive.

I'll let her husband, Andy, take the story from here:

"One day, Jaymie was out driving, and she put the car windows down. It was a windy day, and the wig she was wearing flew right off her head and out the window. She was too embarrassed to go and retrieve it. Instead, she drove to my office, walked in crying, and said, 'I've had a bad day.'

"I looked up at her and said, 'I should say so; you pulled out all of your hair.'

"She laughed. I laughed. It was those kinds of moments that got us through. Today, thank God, Jaymie is completely recovered."

Scared tears

Caroline and Jeff were returning from the doctor's office. She had just learned that the lump in her breast was malignant. Surgery was ahead, followed by chemotherapy and radiation treatments.

As husband and wife drove home, they were upset and scared. Caroline said, "Why did this happen to me? I'm a good and fair person. I've never hurt anyone. I'm a good Catholic. Why would God let this happen to me?"

Jeff shot back, "You? Look what God did to his own son."

There was a moment of silence as Caroline thought about what Jeff said. Then, she started laughing. Even as tears of fear fell on her cheeks, she was laughing. So was Jeff.

"Look honey, maybe it is God's way of bringing you and I closer," said Jeff. "Maybe it's a way to bring the whole family closer. Maybe that's why he let it happen to you."

Caroline shot back, "Well why didn't he let it happen to my brother instead of me?" They laughed again. The more they laughed, the tighter they held each others' hands.

Today, Caroline is free of cancer and Jeff continues to make her laugh.

Boo

Lloyd Arnsmeyer had an abscessed pancreas. It had grown to five times its normal size, and he had a temperature of 104 degrees.

Here's how Lloyd remembers it:

"I was in a great deal of pain. I went to the doctor and told him to cure me or shoot me. Even though the doctor told me I was fine, I overheard him tell my family I might not make it. With all the tubes running out of me, combined with the doctor's unwillingness to tell me the truth, I was fed up.

"I heard the doctor coming down the hall, so I pulled the sheet up over my head. As the doctor walked in, I heard him gasp. He thought I was dead. Just as he reached to pull back the sheet, I screamed out 'Boo!'

"The doctor was so startled, I think he had to change his underwear! After we all had a great laugh, we got down to the business of making me feel better.

"The laughter helped me survive the pain."

They treated us like dogs

Too bad there's not a humor medal in the Armed Services. There are many people who would and should receive it.

Larry Eaton was a POW during the Vietnam War. Two days before he was supposed to head back to the States, he was one of 25 American soldiers captured by the Viet Cong.

Only a half dozen of these men survived the degrading conditions and torture.

"My feet were shackled together, and my hands handcuffed behind my back," Larry said. "They had a chain connecting my hands and feet that ran through my legs. I was put in a hanging cage with no clothing, and I was fed only rice and water. My food was put in a dog dish, and I had to get on all fours and lap it up like a dog. We were treated like dogs and hosed off like dogs.

"One time, I was whispering to a fellow POW about the horrible conditions. He didn't respond. I figured he was too scared to even whisper. I was wrong. He was dead. Once, I had my toenails ripped out with pliers; it was done for my captor's sheer amusement.

"One day, a POW was dragged from his cage and beaten in front of us. While the camp commander was striking him, he lifted his leg and peed on the Viet Cong officer's shoe. The rest of us began to bark and howl like dogs. We laughed, too. We laughed hard.

"We were beaten and punished for our behavior, but we never quit barking and laughing. We laughed every time we thought about it, especially the look on that officer's face when the guy peed on his foot.

"We had to keep our humor. They caged my body, but they couldn't cage my perspective."

What are you doing?

Larry Marks is also a Vietnam veteran.

"Oh there were things around us that were funny," Larry said. "It was always in the middle of something serious. I remember one time we were in a swamp, and there were bullets flying past us from every direction. I wasn't sure we were going to make it this time. I was scared.

"I looked over at another soldier. This guy weighed at least 250 pounds, and he was sitting there in the swamp, covered with frogs. There were about 40 frogs on him, and he was eating a can of peaches.

"I mouthed over to him, 'What are you doing?' He mouthed back, 'I'm hungry.' I laughed very quietly. In the middle of battle, I found humor. It's what kept me going in Vietnam."

Please don't squeeze the charmin

Stephen F. Caruso is a Vietnam veteran who was awarded the Congressional Medal of Honor and received nine other medals and citations for his performance during combat. He also received the Purple Heart for wounds suffered in April of 1968.

Steve enlisted in the Marines and was sent to Vietnam in 1965. He became a scout, someone who would sneak into villages and enemy territory and collect intelligence information. He was involved in some of the most dangerous battle situations in Vietnam.

"I was just an enlisted man who could read a map," Stephen said humbly. "One of my jobs was to confirm the enemy casualties each day. I had to line up the dead bodies. What a way to start or end a day."

With death around him constantly, Steve had to find a way to deal with his emotions. Like many soldiers, he turned to laughter.

"We lived on one can of c-rations a day and one canteen of water," Steve said. "With the poor sanitary conditions and hot, miserable weather, vomiting and diarrhea were an everyday occurrence.

"Our food had to be dropped to us by helicopter. One time, thanks to a typical military mistake, all they gave us were cases of plums. We were so sick of the c-rations that we ate the plums like they were every part of a full-course meal.

"You know plums act like prunes when they are digested. Man, if you thought there was a diarrhea problem before this, triple it! What made it funny was we could only go at night. You have to understand, enemy scouts would watch us all day for any kind of movement, no pun intended. If they saw anything move, they would launch artillery at us. During daylight hours, we were practically frozen into place.

"Now, imagine guys sneaking off at night to do their business. There wasn't enough darkness to accommodate all of our toilet needs. To make it even funnier, our captain ordered an emergency resupply of toilet paper. The helicopter dropped it in this 10-foot-high elephant grass. We had to send out 50 guys to find it.

"The biggest cheer of my duty, no pun intended, came when the toilet paper was being brought into our brigade. You would have thought we won the war that day. Every time I think of that, I laugh."

Lefty and the pit bull

Joseph Pohorence had lymphatic cancer of the tonsils. He beat it with the help of humor. Before every operation and treatment, he would joke around with all of the nurses, even to the point of being obnoxious.

"One time when I was being rushed to hospital in an ambulance the attendant wanted to see if I was still conscious," Joe said. "He asked if I could tell him the name of the President of the United States. I said Hillary Clinton.

"Another time in the operating room, I even got the nurses to joke with me. One asked me if I knew the difference between a woman with PMS and an angry pit bull? Her answer: 'Lipstick.' I loved it. It was the perfect medicine I needed before I went under."

Listen to his plans for his own funeral:

"I told my wife I wanted to record all of my favorite jokes and play them as people walked by my casket. I also wanted one eye open, my tongue hanging out, and one leg draped over the casket. Then, I wanted some device that would spring me up to a sitting position every time someone stepped on a mat."

One of Joe's inspirations was an old boyhood friend, Eddy Peterson, who can find humor in anything. Here's Joe:

"Eddy had a job in a lumber yard. One day, he went to measure a board and accidentally started the saw. The blade severed his right arm.

"When I found out, I rushed to Eddy's side. He was still out of it when I got there. When he finally came to, I began to cry. When I could finally speak, I said, 'I don't know what to say.'

"Eddy looked up at me and said, 'Say what you want, just don't call me Lefty.' That's why I love the guy. Even with an arm cut off he was joking around and making *me* feel better."

It wasn't my time

In these stories, these individuals' names have been changed to protect their identity. These people faced one of the most emotionally wrenching moments in life and, ultimately, laughter helped save and repair their lives.

Randy attempted to kill himself several times. It was his last attempt that he remembers clearly.

"I remember seeing Jesus," Randy told me. "Jesus spoke to me, and told me to go back, that it wasn't my time yet. David, the funny thing is, I'm Jewish. So I definitely knew I still had work to do after that one.

"Since that moment, I find humor everywhere, and I laugh at the outrageousness of my life. It's what gets me through a day and makes it all better. Laughing makes it worth being here."

Sarah also tried to commit suicide. She parked her car in the garage, closed the door, and left the motor running. She told me, "I woke up the next morning and realized I was not dead. And, I was now out of gas and had to walk to a service station to get some. I laughed all the way there, figuring the good Lord wanted me to stick around."

Shrinking leaf

Inspired by his wife's battle with a rare liver disease, Allen Klein wrote the book *The Healing Power of Humor.* Ultimately the disease claimed Ellen Klein's life, but she fought through each day with a smile and a lot of laughs.

Ellen was in the hospital when someone brought her a *Playgirl* magazine, complete with a centerfold poster of a nude male. She hung the centerfold in her room despite Allen's protests; he thought it was too risqué.

To placate him, Ellen told her husband to place a leaf from one of the plants in her room over the private parts of the centerfold model. For several days, this worked well. But the leaf gradually began to shrivel.

I'll let him finish the story:

"Each day we shared a laugh about the leaf gradually revealing the private area of the picture. The laughing only lasted 10 to 20 seconds, but it brought us closer together. It revived us and steered us through our sea of darkness."

The final gift of laughter

Dan Hurst worked in Central America with his parents who were medical missionaries. (Yes, this is the same Dan you previously read about in the family chapter.)

One time when Dan was in Honduras, his parents were tending to an 86-year-old man who was dying. This man wanted to die at home with his family, but his house was in the mountains, several hours away.

Dan agreed to drive this elderly gentleman to his mountain home.

I'll let Dan take the story from here:

"This man had refused to cut his mane of long silver hair. In the jeep, his hair was blowing everywhere. I'm surprised he could see anything. Our ride through the mountains was extremely rough. The roads had many twists and turns, and it was bouncy and uncomfortable. It was also unbearably hot.

"As we arrived at his family's house, the first thing the man said to his family was, 'If you are ever going to die, don't ride in a jeep with Dan Hurst.' Everybody cracked up, especially him.

"The humor did not stop when the man passed away. As the pallbearers carried his casket through the streets of his small town, the family followed behind. I remember as we approached a steep hill to the gravesite, his widow began to laugh. Then, everyone in the procession began to laugh.

"The man's long silver hair was hanging out of the back of the casket. They had closed the lid without placing all of his hair inside. His widow said: 'I told him to cut that hair. Even at his funeral, he still makes me laugh.'"

Get well soon

After one of my talks on the **humor perspective**, a man shared this story with me. Humor helped him through one of the most uncomfortable moments of his life, a time when he thought a friend was dying.

"I was nervously waiting to see one my best friends. He was in the hospital after having his leg amputated because of diabetes. My anxiety reached its peak as I walked into his room.

"I was surprised to find him laughing with a nurse. Here I was nervous and scared, and he was in a great mood. As I approached him I stuttered, stammered, and said, 'I'm kind of surprised you are in such good spirits. I wasn't sure how you'd be doing.'

"My friend said, 'How could I not be in a good mood when friends send you cards like this one.' The card read: 'Hope you'll soon be well and back on your feet.' The person who sent the card had crossed out feet and written 'foot.'"

Every story in this book touched a unique emotional core in me; that's why I chose them. The following story touched me deeply. Maybe it's because I saw how courage and humor put a cream pie right in death's face.

In his published work, *Faith After The Holocaust*, philosopher Eliezer Berkowitz recounts the following story. It is about a nameless Jewish woman in the Maidanek Nazi concentration camp, near Lublin, Poland. Together with her sister, she tried to escape. The sister escaped; she was caught.

The gallows were set up in the center of the commando square so all could witness. As the hangman and the victim stood on the gallows, the hangman spoke first.

"Who helped you to get away?" he asked.

"A Jewess does not betray those who tried to help her," she replied.

"Don't you see how everybody laughs at you?" said the German. "You are beautiful. One name, one word could save you. And the world is delightful."

The woman's final words were, "Today you laugh, tomorrow you will be laughed at."

Chapter 9

You Just Have to Laugh... Even If You're Famous

Well-known people must suffer through life's trials and tribulations just like the rest of us. And just like anybody else, celebrities—whether they're athletes, entertainers, politicians, or authors—can use humor to help them through trying times.

This chapter is dedicated to people who not only have names you'll recognize, but also a **humorous perspective** that you may not have known about. Part of their formula for success is laughter, even when it means laughing at themselves.

As you'll see in this first story, not only can humor push you through physical barriers, it can break down the walls of bigotry as well.

Happy endings aren't just for movies

When movie maker Steven Spielberg was a teenager, his family moved to Northern California. It was at his new high school that he ran into anti-Semitism.

As the story goes, some of his new classmates would cough the word "Jew" when they passed him in the halls. One bully compounded the abuse by regularly hitting him during flag football games in gym class.

Just before graduation, Steven filmed the senior-class excursion to Santa Cruz. While shooting footage on the trip, he asked several students, including the bully and his buddies, to look up and flinch. He asked others to put their hands over their eyes.

When the film was shown at graduation, there was a scene of a sea gull flying overhead. Into this scene, Steven had spliced shots of the bully and his friends touching their faces as if they had been splattered by the passing bird.

Steven expected the bully to be furious with his creative editing, but the opposite happened. The bully told him his movie was good and that he was a funny guy. The bully also told him he wished he would have gotten to know Steven better, and he apologized for his meanness.

Steven Spielberg learned a familiar lesson to many of us—one of the best ways to handle the bullies of the world is with laughter.

Drop Pheidippides ... drop

Frank Shorter has been a world-class distance runner most of his life. He won the gold medal at the Summer Olympic Games in 1972 and came back four years later and took the silver. He continues to set record times for distance races in his age group.

The marathon is the most grueling of athletic events. It covers more than 26 miles and is a test of physical and mental endurance. As Frank Shorter discovered, it also requires a dose of humor.

"One of my first competitive marathons was at the Pan Am Games," Frank said. "I have to first give you some background about the history of the marathon. According to legend, around 490 B.C., an Athenian general dispatched Pheidippides, a runner messenger, to Sparta.

"Supposedly, Pheidippides ran a route that took

him south along the coast and across a series of coastal foothills before descending into Athens, a distance of about 26 miles. When he arrived in Athens, Pheidippides announced, 'Rejoice. We conquer!' Then, he fell dead.

"Well, during my first marathon at the Pan Am Games, I hit what is called the 'wall' at the 20-mile mark. (The wall is a point in the marathon where the runners don't feel like they can go on, either physically or mentally.)

"At the time I hit the wall, I was tied for first place. I looked at the runner next to me and said, 'Man, I wish Pheidippides would have dropped dead at the 20-mile mark.'

"It made me laugh. It relaxed me. I didn't win the race, but it helped get me through the wall and finish second place. That qualified me for my first spot on the U.S. Olympic team."

Mr. Warmth

Comedian Don Rickles is known as the king of put-downs. In Las Vegas, people flock to his show, not only to see him, but to become part of his routine.

This particular evening, Don was 30 minutes into his act when a man and woman were escorted to the front row of the theater. Mr. Putdown stopped and acknowledged the couple's entrance.

"Hey, Mr. and Mrs. Hockey Puck, you're 30 minutes late," Rickles said.

The man shot back, "No, we're early. You're still on."

Don literally dropped to his knees laughing. The man received a standing ovation for his comeback while Mr. Putdown laughed so hard he was crying.

We miss you, Jimmy V

The late Jimmy Valvano was an exceptional human being as well as a great college basketball coach.

Once during a very spirited and tense game, Coach Valvano and one of the officials argued constantly. Jimmy V was hit with a technical foul, and the official warned him to keep his mouth shut or he would kick him out of the game.

As he paced the sidelines, Coach Valvano suffered through several more of what he considered to be lousy calls. During a time-out, he asked the official, "Can I get kicked out of the game for what I'm thinking?"

The unsuspecting official told him no.

That's when Jimmy V shot back with a smile on his face: "I think your officiating sucks tonight."

The referee started laughing. Jimmy V laughed. From that point on, every time they looked at each other, they laughed again.

Taking you higher

Gloria Estefan is one of the most popular singers in the world. When she goes on tour, it's always a big production.

During one of her concerts in Holland, she was suspended above the stage in what appeared to be a large steel ball. As she started singing her song "Higher," the ball was supposed to ascend into the air.

But suddenly, the ball stopped. Gloria continued to sing about going higher, but the ball did not move.

Instead of getting flustered, Gloria had fun with the moment by singing: "I think I'm stuck in the ball now."

Eventually, she had to be pulled out of the ball and lowered to the stage. But her willingness to laugh at the glitch made for a memorable moment for her audience.

Sorry about that

Chris Syfert is an auto racing enthusiast. Several years ago, she was working with a racing team whose car had a new engine. A crazy Dutchman named Jan (pronounced "yawn") Lammers was the driver.

I will let Chris take it from here:

"This was the final race of the season, and our chief engineer was wound pretty tight. Everyone was edgy about the new engine, and his attitude didn't make it any easier.

"On the pace lap, Jan got the car up to speed but

came over the radio saying he had a problem. Everyone on the headsets tensed up. The chief engineer asked him what was wrong.

"I think I just started my period," Jan said.

"We all broke out laughing. We knew he was a crazy guy, but this took the cake. It put all of us in a great frame of mind, and even loosened up the chief engineer.

"Later on, Jan was leading the race and was hit by another driver. The car spun around and was going backward down the main straightaway. Jan was actually driving by looking in his rearview mirror. Once he was through the straightaway, he did a perfect 180 degree turn and got back in the race, regaining his lead.

"He came on the radio and said, 'Sorry about that.' We all started laughing again.

"I'm convinced we won the race that day because that crazy Dutchman kept us all loose with his sense of humor."

Nobody knows the trouble I've seen

Robert Donner is an actor who has appeared in numerous television shows, including starring roles on "The Waltons" and "Mork & Mindy." When faced with one of life's most threatening situations, Robert responded with humor.

I'll let him tell the story:

"One morning, I was in bed and felt the pressure of a hundred pound bag of rocks on my chest and a burning sensation up and down my left arm. I told my wife she had better call a doctor.

"As I laid there waiting for the ambulance, I thought, 'This isn't going to be a very good day.' Ten minutes later, the paramedics arrived with a gurney. One of the guys had a mustache with about five hairs in it and acted as if he had never worked a gurney before. He came right out of a Three Stooges bit.

"As Mo and Larry lifted me on the gurney, a wheel fell off. One guy was balancing the gurney while the other crawled under the bed to retrieve the wheel. During this entire fiasco, my wife was clutching the dog while sitting on the bed singing, 'Nobody knows the trouble I've seen.'

"Once they got me to the hospital, they did not know what floor the intensive care unit was on. The two stooges ended up arguing as they tried every one of the building's three floors.

"Eight days later, I woke up. I had suffered a heart attack. If it wasn't for the humorous order of events that distracted me, I'm not sure I would have gotten through the experience.

"Now, when I remember my heart attack, I laugh."

Batter up

(Let me know if you know which great pitcher this story's about; I honestly can't remember.)

There was a major league baseball pitcher who not only could throw the ball but also had the gift of throwing off opposing batters using humor.

On one occasion, a batter took his stance, looked at the pitcher, and made the sign of the cross.

The pitcher immediately stepped off the mound, crossed himself, pointed at the batter, and said, "OK, pal, it's just between you and me, now."

Superman don't need a seat belt

In this classic story, it was a flight attendant who brought down the great boxer Muhammad Ali.

As the jet was rolling down to the runway, the flight attendant instructed the heavyweight champion that he needed to fasten his seat belt. He looked at her, smiled and said, "Superman don't need a seat belt."

She gave an even bigger smile and said, "No, Superman don't need an airplane. Will you buckle up please?"

Ali laughed as he fastened his seat belt.

Dara-ducky, you're the one

Dara Torres was a member of the U.S. Swimming Team for the 1984, 1988, and 1992 Summer Olympic Games. She was the first American swimmer to earn medals in three consecutive Olympics.

Dara won the gold medal in the 400-meter freestyle at the 1992 Games in Barcelona, and she remembers the events leading up to that race.

"There was a waiting room where all of the competitors gathered before the race," Dara said. "All of the girls were sitting there, either staring straight ahead or attempting to intimidate their opponents by staring at them. I walked into the room last with my walkman blasting, and I screamed, 'What's up everybody?'

"Once we got out to the pool, I jumped in the water. It was very cold, so I wanted to get used to it by splashing water on me. Since I was the only one in the water, it was easy to notice all of my competitors glaring at me with 'intimidating eyes.' I began to spit water into their lanes just for fun. It made me laugh and eased my prerace tension.

"I felt good and relaxed on the starting block because I laughed and was silly. It worked. I won the gold medal."

Her friends are the true gold

Janet Evans was a member of the United States swimming team in the 1988, 1992 and 1996 Summer Olympic Games. She won five gold medals and 45 national titles. She is the only female swimmer to hold world records in three distances concurrently—the 400-meter, 800-meter, and 1,600-meter freestyle races.

Janet has been competing since she was a child. When I asked her if humor had helped her, she told me the following:

"As a kid, my friends would always say, 'Don't get caught in the lane lines.' Those are the ropes that divide the lanes in the pool. That was our ongoing joke for years. No matter the competition, that comment was always their way of wishing me good luck.

"My last Olympics in 1996, I didn't do as well as I wanted. I was disappointed and sad. When my friends met me at the airport, the first thing they said was, 'Well, at least you didn't get your foot caught in the lane line.'

"They knew what I needed. That was just the thing I needed to hear. It made me smile, laugh, and even gave me a lump in my throat. They're the best friends a person could have."

No Mr. Ordinary

In the book *Ronald Reagan: How an Ordinary Man Became An Extraordinary Leader*, author Dinesh D'Souza shared the following story.

During a summit meeting with Russian leader Mikhail Gorbachev, President Reagan tried to lighten the mood with a joke:

"An American and Russian were arguing. The American said, 'Look I can go into the Oval Office, pound the president's desk and say, 'Mr. President, I don't like the way you're running our country.'"

The Russian responded, "I can do that too."

The American said, "You can?"

"Sure," said the Russian. "I can go into the general secretary's office in the Kremlin and say: 'Mr. General Secretary, I don't like the way that President Reagan is running his country.'"

Are you OK, Floyd?

Competing at the highest level of athletics requires an incredible degree of physical talent, dedication, and the ability to overcome mistakes. Sometimes the best way to do that is with laughter.

Floyd Little was an All-American running back at Syracuse University who went on to play professionally for the Denver Broncos.

He told me the following story:

"Dick Butkus of the Chicago Bears was one of the hardest hitting linebackers in football history. As a running back, you could never let the opposing team know they hurt you with a hard hit. One time, I got hit harder by Mr. Butkus than I can ever remember. He hit me so hard I don't think there was any fluid left in my body.

"I didn't want to let him know how bad he shook me up, so I got up and said, 'Is that all you got? Was that your best hit?' Butkus just looked at me and said, 'You all right, Little?'

"I answered by saying, 'I thought you were a hard hitter, man.' Again he asked me if I was OK.

"So I said, 'Why do you keep asking me that man?'

"Butkus looked at me with a smirk and said, 'Because you're in the wrong huddle, Floyd.'"

Just because you are famous doesn't mean you don't have to deal with tragedy or fear. Even celebrities have learned to deal with the lighter side of a dark situation.

> "If you can find humor in anything, you can
>   survive it."
>
> *Bill Cosby*

I discovered this quote from Bill Cosby one year before his son, Ennis, was murdered on a Los Angeles freeway. During this most difficult time, Bill showed us that humor and laughter are always appropriate.

He told the following story one night on CNN's "The Larry King Show" how the family gathered at the grave site, holding hands and each other. They shared stories about Ennis. The stories moved from truthful accounts to humorous memories. Their tears moved to smiles, then to laughs that moved to healing.

Bill told his brother that they walked and carried Ennis down the hill to his grave, almost as slaves. After they laughed, the walk up the hill was lighter and felt more free.

In an interview with Dan Rather in the days following the funeral, Bill said he drove to work every day and saw people looking at him with sadness. He said what we all needed was to laugh again.

I have heard Bill brag about how Ennis was his role model and how proud he was of him.

I am sure as he looks down from heaven, Ennis is proud of his father.

I am Henry Kissinger

In 1994, the United States was the host country for the World Cup Soccer competition. The U.S. team won more games and went farther than anyone expected. Goalkeeper Tony Meola thinks the success came because the team stayed loose and laughed together.

Tony took me behind the scenes, telling this story:

"What really set the humorous tone for our team happened right before our first game. Former Secretary of State Henry Kissinger was instrumental in getting the World Cup to the United States, and he wanted to meet us in the locker room.

"Keep in mind, he was secretary of state before most of our team was born. When a team official came in and told us Mr. Kissinger wanted to meet the team, my teammate Alexi Lalas said, 'Who the hell is Henry Kissinger?'

"A man behind him said, 'I am Henry Kissinger.' The room erupted in laughter. It continued as we ran on the field and during our warm-up period. Every time we passed one another, we would say, 'I am Henry Kissinger.' Every time we said it, we laughed.

"It kept us loose."

Julia/Pat? We still love you

Julia Sweeney is a former cast member of the television show "Saturday Night Live." She created the androgynous and memorable character Pat. The movie she created, made by the same name, received bad reviews and was immediately moved to video.

The same time her movie was disappearing from theaters, her brother Mike was told he had lymphoma. Julia was taking care of him when, just weeks before his death in April, 1995, Julia was diagnosed with cervical cancer.

The two of them shared a hospital room. During their treatment together, Mike would answer the phone "International House of Cancer."

Three days after her brother's death, Julia had a hysterectomy. Her doctor suggested they could harvest eggs from her still-functioning ovaries, which could later be fertilized by a sperm donor. Later, the egg could be carried to term by a surrogate mother.

Julia's response to this?

"Oh great, now I have to meet a guy and a girl."

I need to see a priest

Ernie Stautner is a pro football hall of famer who is known for his toughness. Ernie is the kind of guy that people will be telling stories about as long as humans walk upright. When I met him, he insisted he had a story for me. From his mouth to you:

"I can't tell you how many times in my 14-year career in the NFL that I needed a shot of pain-killing Novocaine just to keep me going. I've had broken ribs, a cracked sternum, and seven broken noses. My knees were twisted like pretzels. I crushed the carpel tunnel bones in both hands. I broke my thumb once during a game, and the bone was sticking out of the skin with blood all over my uniform. My teammates were in shock when I stuck the bone back into the skin, walked back into the huddle, looked at our defensive captain, and casually said, 'OK, what's the defense for this play?' I guess you could say pain is an old friend of mine.

"One game, I died right before the kickoff and somehow lived to tell about it. I was mistakenly given the very powerful sedative Demerol, instead of Novocaine. In fact, I was given 1,200 milligrams—enough to knock out a horse.

"Four hours later, I couldn't tell if I was awake or dreaming. A nurse was holding an oxygen mask over my mouth shouting, 'Breathe! Breathe, dammit, breathe!' I found out later they were injecting me with a drug to counteract the Demerol.

"My eyes opened, and I was looking at the holes in the white ceiling tile. One of the doctors approached me and said, 'Are you awake? Do you know who you are?'

"Yeah, I think I'm Ernie Stautner," I answered.

"Looking puzzled, the doctor continued, 'Do you know what you were supposed to do today?'

"Yeah," I said, "I was supposed to beat the snot out of the Cleveland Browns. But somehow, doc, I don't think I made it.

"He walked over to a group of doctors. They were whispering, so I was sure something must be wrong.

"Give me a priest," I shouted at the doctor.

Suddenly, I wanted to fall back asleep; the nurse was still standing over me, yelling 'Breathe, dammit, breathe!' I was thinking about giving up when the priest arrived and said, 'They say you think you are going to die.'

"Yeah, father, it's true. I need to say my last confession. Father bless me, for I have sinned.

"I was feeling dizzy and the room was starting to move. The hazy white light was growing darker. Doctors were over in the corner whispering about me.

"Excuse me, father," I continued, "You see, I don't have much time. Is all right with you, father, if I just hit the highlights?"

Chapter 10

You Just
Have to Laugh...

And These People Prove It

I'm happy to say this chapter is about some friends of mine. They are humor warriors. They are the kind of people that make this world a better place.

Are you real?

Jo Bonewits has many interests—art (especially pottery), teaching, and the work she does as the director of a doll and miniature museum.

But Jo's eyes sparkle the brightest when she talks about clowning. I'll let her explain what it does for others and, especially, what it does for her:

"I was at a children's hospital clowning when I heard a little boy crying. He had broken his arm and was screaming out in pain.

"When he saw me, he got quiet. I told him he was like a car that was broken, and then I took out my teddy bear puppet who told the little boy, 'I want to give you some love.' He let the puppet kiss him while I continued to praise him for being a good boy. He talked freely with the puppet, forgetting about his pain. He was even smiling and waving goodbye as he was wheeled off to X-ray.

"There was also the time I was clowning around at another hospital with a girl who spoke no English. She had been abused and I could see the bruises on her body. It broke my heart. We played together, being silly, laughing, and clowning around, breaking the language barrier between us.

"As I left her, my heart felt good to see her smile,

and I prayed her smiles would stay.

"When I'm clowning, I always let people come to me. I never force myself on them. Once, I stood at the door of a patient's room in an adult ward in my full clown costume and asked, 'Who needs some cheering up? Would anybody like some company?'

"A woman in bed said, 'Are you real?'

"I said, 'I'm your best dream or your worst nightmare.' The woman smiled and asked if she could touch me. I held her hand and she said, 'You are real.' I told her of course I was real, and asked her why she doubted that.

"The woman smiled and said softly, 'They've been giving me a lot of drugs, and I have been seeing things. I can't wait to tell the doctor my hallucinations became real.'

"I'll never forget an older woman named Rita so weakened by her condition that she couldn't get out of bed and lay in the fetal position.

"I moved her bed ever so slightly and said softly, 'Rita? Rita? I brought some sunshine for you today.'

"She opened one eye and saw me in my full clown makeup. She just stared. I asked her if she was OK. She answered, 'Oh my, look at the sunshine in here. It's not outside. It's all in here.'

"A nurse slowly helped her get up. When she finally moved by herself, I asked, 'Are you going to stay up all day and enjoy the sunshine in here.'

"Rita looked right at me, smiled, and said, 'I think I'll live today.'

"That's why I do it. It's just as healing for me as it is for them."

I never took it that seriously

Bob Wieland lost his legs in the Vietnam War. That tragedy hardly slowed him down; his accomplishments are truly incredible.

He walked across the United States on his arms and bottom! Bob started in 1982 and finished his journey across America in 1986—three years, eight months, and six days later.

Bob has competed in Hawaii in the Ironman Triathlon, a two-mile ocean swim, followed by a 112-mile bicycle ride, followed by a full 26-mile marathon. It took him three days without sleep, but he finished.

People magazine once honored Bob as one of the most amazing Americans. He was a former strength coach for the Green Bay Packers and a former world record holder in the bench press, once lifting 507 pounds.

Now, Bob works as a motivational speaker, and, one day, he and I shared the same stage. Watching him speak, I wondered if he had a story for my book. I thought surely he had used humor at sometime during his challenges.

He thought for only a couple of seconds, and then said with his trademark smirk, "You know, David, I never took it too seriously that I lost my legs."

Quite honestly, I was looking for a bigger and better story. Bob told me he would think about it, and I should call him. For two months, we played phone tag and never connected.

Then one day it hit me; I already had the story. "I never took it too seriously that I lost my legs."

Not taking his condition seriously moved him to greatness. Bob Weiland, with his lighthearted spirit and physical triumphs, is a true role model for everyone.

Do yourself a favor. If you have a chance to see Bob speak or purchase one of his books, please do. I guarantee your life, spirit, and faith in humanity will soar. Bob Weiland will walk you to the heights of your soul.

Miles

Miles Postlethwait was born five weeks ahead of his expected due date. Born on a Wednesday, he underwent his first operation on Friday, two days later.

He suffered from many congenital birth defects. He was born without an anus. He had a congenital heart disease. Miles spent most of his first 45 days on a respirator and weighed just four pounds. When his parents took him home, they had to buy doll clothes to dress him, because he was so small.

Miles has had bladder problems, kidney stones, and has worn a colostemy bag for six years. He's had a hernia and an enlarged spleen. During the first six years of his life, Miles has had 39 operations!

I sat in the living room of Eric and Marty Postlethwait, comforted by a La-Z-Boy rocker and a warm fire. Marty sat in her rocker, while Eric and Miles were stretched out on the couch. Daughter Melissa was in the kitchen, still in her basketball uniform as she did her homework. Another daughter, Mallory, sat in a chair by the fire.

I came to this happy home to ask Eric and Marty whether at any time during Miles' ordeal humor had saved the day.

"Oh heavens yes," said Marty. "On about the 30th operation, Miles got sick every time they put the anesthesia mask over his mouth. Miles laid on his hospital bed and politely said, 'No mask. If you let me lay here for a while, I'll just fall asleep on my own.' This cracked up all the doctors and made everyone laugh, including Miles. It made him relax before his surgery.

"We all have become silly throughout time. At first, we were too serious, and that didn't help Miles or our other kids. My husband and I spent every night in the hospital for two years. Finally, one of the nurses suggested we do split shifts, so we could spend more time at home.

"We started communicating with each other by writing notes on Miles' diaper. We would write instructions or just thoughts of affection. It was fun. A lot of times, it was the relief we needed.

"My friend, Karen, also had a child in the same hospital. One night she took me for a ride around the hospital in a kid's wagon. We both needed to laugh and get silly."

Miles also has a sense of humor. Once he was asked to be the poster child for a high school all-star game. He posed for a picture with Bill Maas, who was then playing in the NFL for the Kansas City Chiefs. Miles sat on Bill's shoulder but was getting very antsy and was also in a great deal of pain. To get him to continue, Bill offered him a dollar to keep going.

Miles looked at him and said, "Is that all? Just one dollar?"

"Early on," Marty said, "we adopted that old philosophy of when life throws you lemons, make lemonade. More than half of the marriages of chronically ill children end in divorce. Eric and I were determined not to let that happen.

"By keeping everything light, I know it was easier for Miles and us, too. We decided, 'Let's laugh,' because if we didn't, it would drive us crazy and we'd be constantly depressed."

As I was saying my goodbyes, Miles had answered the phone and told his older sister it was for her. She picked it up, but he stayed on the phone, listening to her conversation, and laughing. From the other room, his sister started yelling for him to hang up. That made him laugh even more.

At face value, the Postlethwaits look like a normal, happy-go-lucky family. One might never know what they have been through and only the good Lord knows what the future has in store. Yet, as I drove away, I had the distinct impression they would get through it, finding humor along the way.

9,000 to go

W. Mitchell has a remarkable resume. He's a self-made millionaire, respected environmentalist, sought-after speaker, former mayor of Denver, and congressional candidate. He enjoys river rafting and sky diving.

Mitchell did all of this after two horrific accidents; the second one was a plane crash that left him a paraplegic. The first one came when he was riding his motorcycle and collided with a laundry truck. When the cycle went down, it crushed his elbow and fractured his pelvis. The gas tank ruptured and the leaking gasoline ignited, burning him over 64 percent of his body. If it wasn't for a passerby who put out the flames with a fire extinguisher, Mitchell would not be alive today.

His face had been burned off. His fingers were charred and twisted. His legs were nothing but raw, red flesh. Some visitors seeing him for the first time fainted. He was unconscious for two weeks.

During a period of four months he had 13 transfusions, 16 skin graft operations, and other surgeries. There was a moment when Mitchell says humor saved his life.

"It was actually my plastic surgeon who created this moment," he said. "When we met to talk about the surgery he would do on my face, he asked me if I had a picture of myself before the accident. I gave him my driver's license.

"The doctor studied it, then looked at me and

said, 'Oh heck, I can do better than that.' I started laughing. It brought me out of myself and put me on the road to recovery—just by laughing."

Vinnie

Vinnie Vaccaro is the former president of the Kansas City chapter of the Dream Factory, the organization that fulfills the dreams and wishes of seriously ill children.

That alone tells you a lot about Vinnie. But it doesn't give you the full picture of this man who has the will of a bull and the heart of the late Mother Theresa.

He shared a story with me that I want to share with you. But, I have to put a warning label on it. Some people may find the language offensive. Personally, I think to change the words would take away the honesty of the situation in this story. Out of respect to my readers, I wanted to give fair warning.

Vinnie was married in August of 1968. One week later his father died of a heart attack. Three months later, his new bride died in an automobile accident, and Vinnie sat at the funeral home, surrounded by his family. I'll let Vinnie take the story from here:

"Forget the Irish, nobody mourns like an Italian. Nobody hurts like we do. Nobody makes as much noise as we do. Here I am, 21 years old, and I just lost the person who was the center of my universe. I was surrounded by grieving family and friends, when in walks an old friend of mine, Steve Caruso. (Steve appears in chapter 8.)

"Steve is a decorated Vietnam veteran, a magna cum laude graduate of the University of California-Berkeley Law School, where he was Phi Beta Kappa. Not only is he book smart, he's street smart. Steve has never allowed himself to take anything seriously and has tried to make sure his friends don't either.

"He walked in, came right over to me, smiled, and said, 'So, Vinnie, what the fuck's going on?'

"He looked around and said, 'What are you doing here? This place is depressing.'

"All of a sudden, I started laughing. Steve continued, saying 'Let's get out of here and get some coffee.' The next thing I know, I'm in the basement of this funeral home, drinking coffee, eating doughnuts, and laughing my head off as Steve tells stories about law school.

"I can remember very few things about that week of my life. I remember identifying my wife's body. I remember picking out the dress she would be buried in. I can remember the hurt. But mostly, I remember that Steve Caruso had me laughing. He knew the prescription I needed to help me get on with my life."

Joey

Joey Plesser was born April 10, 1964. It didn't take long for doctors to discover Joey was suffering from the disease neurofibromatosis, more commonly called "Elephant Man's Disease," which causes tumors, sometimes cancerous, all over the body.

I've known the Plesser family for years since they used to live down the street from my aunt and uncle. One day I sat down with Joey's parents, Carole and Stan, so they could share stories with me about their son. I told them I was always amazed that Joey was able to laugh despite his condition.

Although he had thousands of tumors all over his body, Stan told me Joey was never embarrassed by them.

"When Joey was younger, he told me, 'Dad, it's OK if people stare. They aren't being mean. They're just curious. Heck, I'd stare too, if I saw somebody who looked like me'."

Carole said, "One of the doctors who was studying Joey's disease told us that for some reason a lot of people who have neurofibromatosis have a high degree of genius. They are also very creative and have a great sense of humor. Joey was aware of his gift and loved to draw, write, and make up stories to the point of driving us crazy.

"Every time we asked him if there was an ending coming soon to one of his stories, he would miraculously tie it all to together, making us laugh.

"Joey was always ready to be funny. One time, I remember some kid looked at him and said, 'You're really ugly.' Joey smiled and said, 'You may be right. On the outside I may be ugly. But you're ugly on the inside.'"

At the age of 12, Joey created a cartoon character named, 'Laser Boy.'

"Keep in mind, this was before laser light shows and laser guns were around," said Stan. "He created entire stories about Laser Boy and other characters, including the neighborhood kids in his many productions.

"One time, I asked him if God gave him the choice of being a perfectly healthy kid with a not-so-creative mind, or of being exactly the way he was, what would he choose? Joey said he would choose to be exactly the way he was."

Carole continued, "With Joey's disease, there was always the chance he could become deaf, blind, or that any number of other complications could set in. The worst complication was cancer. I remember one day he was feeling very depressed. I told him I thought he had two roads he could travel.

"The first road was to stay miserable. He could continue being sad and feeling sorry for himself. The other road was to be happy, enjoy himself, and simply accept it. Both roads came with his disease, so as I saw it, there really wasn't a choice.

"He looked at me intently and took in every word. It's one of the few times I can remember him being quiet."

In the fall of 1980, Joey developed cancer. He became bedridden and his parents had to turn him every 20 minutes and help with his feeding and toilet needs. On Thanksgiving Day, Joey stopped breathing. Carole had to resuscitate him before the ambulance showed up and took him to the hospital.

"By the time I got to see him in the hospital, he

was hooked up to a machine with tubes going in and out of him to help him breathe and eat," Carole said. "When I walked in the room and saw all of these tubes in my son, I said to him, 'Well you finally did it Joey ... up your nose with a rubber hose.'

"He was barely conscious, but he looked at me and smiled. He loved that I made a joke, especially at a time like that."

Several months later, Joey was back home and his family held a birthday party for him. One of the guests was John Dillon, a member of the singing group Ozark Mountain Daredevils. Stan Plesser was the manager for the group and several other rock 'n' roll acts.

"John came up from Arkansas to see Joey," said Stan. "Joey used to give John a hard time about being from Arkansas. He would say things like, 'Do they have phones yet down there? How about cars? How did you get up here, by horse?' It got to be a running joke with them.

"This was about the time the hostages were freed from Iran, right around the time when Ronald Reagan became president. John stood at the door of Joey's room, and Joey, who was very weak and could barely talk, waved at John to come closer.

"John leaned down and Joey told him, 'Hey John, I thought you'd like to know that they freed the hostages.'

"It was amazing that during his weakest moment, he still took the time to bust on John. He didn't let his condition get him down. We would not have the perspective we have if it wasn't for Joey's attitude. He was a gift for 17 years."

Joey Plesser died on April 27, 1981. Stan said Joey always told him that if he died, he would come back and visit them. He believed in life after death.

"Steve (another son) and I were in his room when Joey died," said Stan. "He looked at Steve and then he looked at me with that big smile of his. Then, he died. He was letting us know that he was OK and not to worry because he was going to be just fine."

Carole showed me some of Joey's writings and drawings. We all laughed at the certificate he created for kids who got caught skipping school. He even made certificates for kids who got in trouble with the police.

But it was what Carole showed me next that touched me most deeply. When Joey was in grade school, he passed out handmade business cards like the one Carole showed me. It read:

Joey Plesser
"Genius"

I don't know if Joey has come back to visit his family like he said he would. I do know Joey Plesser is very much alive in the hearts and memory of his parents. He is still making them laugh.

"Joey did not like for me to hold his hand when we went into stores," Carole told me as I was leaving. "It seemed like within seconds he would scatter, and in minutes I would hear over the intercom, 'Would the parents of Joey Plesser please pick him up at the customer service counter. He is lost'."

Stan said, "He loved the attention. He loved to hear his name over the loudspeaker. When we'd go and get him he would always be standing there smiling."

There are angels amongst us

Not all angels have wings, play the harp, and drift the day away on white puffy clouds. They live amongst us, and when you find one, you'll know. Meet Connie and Bill Wahl.

I met them while working on the cruise ship, the S.S. Norway. I was sitting by the pool, talking with a friend of mine, cracking some jokes. That's when I noticed Connie and Bill laughing, too. We all shared some conversation before saying our goodbyes and heading off to dinner.

I watched as Connie helped Bill who struggled to stand. It was the first time I noticed he had trouble moving. I learned later he suffers from muscular dystrophy.

Showing her sense of humor, Connie calls her husband "Wiglet" because he shakes when he walks and moves.

"Connie has always been outgoing, fun, silly, and louder than my family," said Bill. "They accepted her but still weren't quite sure how to take her.

"Connie's dad, on the other hand, is a card. He told me that Connie was a good choice to marry because she had great teeth; he would guarantee them.

Last year, the cost of Connie's root canal came to more than $2,000, so I called Connie's dad and asked about those guaranteed teeth. He said, 'Sorry the warranty ran out,' and hung up the phone laughing."

Bill has lived with his muscular dystrophy for 16 years, and there have been many trying moments. "I remember one year where Connie had to give me a shot once a day," Bill said.

Connie jumped in, "It was testosterone. We were busy that year." They both started laughing.

Bill isn't the only one with physical problems; Connie suffers from diabetes. She told me a story about the time she was taken to the hospital emergency room in a coma.

"In my coma, I went to this place where the joy was unbelievable," she said. "It was a thousand times better than any Christmas or any picnic. There was just unbelievable joy. I remember saying, "This is wonderful," and a voice saying to me, 'This is nothing. Do you want to stay?' And when I said I did, the voice asked, 'What about Bill and the children?' That's when I said, 'No, I'll leave.'

"That's when I heard the doctor say, 'Well, she'll be dead or brain damaged with that blood sugar level.'

"I immediately sat right up on the table and said, 'You should never say that in front of a patient. I'm getting out of here.'"

At Bill and Connie's request, I spent a couple days hanging out with them on the cruise. Let me share with you some of the things I observed:

I sat with Bill on the beach as he struggled to light his pipe, feed himself, and try to stand. When he missed his mouth with a nacho chip, spilling it all over his shirt, he looked at Connie and said, "Here's another one for the cleaners, Mom."

As I pushed him along the sand in a wheelchair, he said, "Don't you wish this thing had a turbocharger?"

Watching his wife lumber to the water and dive in, Bill said, "Isn't she wonderful."

One night after dinner on the Norway, Bill was using his cane to walk away from the table and fell down. As Connie helped him up, he said, "Tell the captain not to move the ship like that again."

During that cruise, I never heard a moan, a groan, or a complaint. There was always a smile, a thank you, a laugh, or a funny comment. Bill never appeared fazed or disillusioned, and Connie was always right there to support, help, and laugh.

"Oh, there have been some tough times," Bill told me. "But thanks to Connie and our kids, and a lot of humor, it's been a lot easier. It's been our laughing that has gotten us through it."

I have no doubt there are angels amongst us. How we find them is up to us. But I can tell you this, if you ever smell pipe smoke, hear a woman gently call "Wiglet" and laugh, then get your camera out because you've found a couple of angels named Connie and Bill.

And you think you've had a bad day

Charlie Plumb was a prisoner of war in Vietnam. As a POW, Charlie was tortured and nearly beaten to death for information about American troop movements. Sometimes Charlie was beaten because his captors got drunk and thought it was fun.

Charlie recalls the first time he was beaten and tortured. He felt like he was near death. As he lay on the cold concrete, barely able to open his eyes, he saw something scrawled along the bottom of a wall.

The words were written in English and provided Charlie Plumb with the humorous relief he so needed at this most difficult moment. Imprisoned in this room of torture, barely holding onto life, this is what Charlie saw:

Smile, you're on candid camera.

Final Thoughts

Writing this book has changed me. I have looked into the eyes of people who have faced death, and they continued to laugh and enjoy their existence. I have looked into the eyes of people who have lost loved ones, and they still find a smile and a laugh. I have seen and heard laughter where I never would have believed it existed.

Through their laughter, I've come to appreciate my life and the ups and downs it brings me. When I start to whine or feel sorry for myself, I only have to think about some of the people in this book.

One day Rabbi Paul Levenson had me do the following exercise. Why don't you try it? Imagine you're on your death bed with friends and family gathered around. Before you die, tell them what you learned in your life. Here's what I came up with:

"Enjoy yourself. Do what you love. Surround yourself with joy because when you get down to it, what else is there? Since we are here occupying time, enjoy every second of it."

I love being a comedian. I am proud that I chose comedy as a profession, passion, and avocation. I love making people laugh, and I enjoy laughing myself. I love what laughing does to human beings. I especially love original comedians and their unique perspectives on any given subject, especially when they poke fun at the serious stuff in life. They also show us that we can laugh at our differences.

On the surface, who could be more different than a musician and a scientist? One approaches their work and passion from the different hemispheres of the brain. Yet the great musician Pablo Casals and the great scientist Albert Schweitzer both believed they lived to their mid-90s because of humor and music.

They would listen every day to some of their favorite musical passages, and found humor in their daily routines. Both stated they felt more restored, regenerated, and enhanced by a laugh and their favorite music.

So take a tip from the masters—listen to your favorite music and go have a good laugh!

Some people have a hard time finding the enjoyment and the humorous angle to the world around them. I offer this suggestion: Take a step back and attempt to appreciate the comic twist whenever you can. If people could laugh while they were going through the Holocaust, if they can laugh while suffering from a terminal disease, if people can laugh their way out of suicide, then I believe anything is laughable.

Finding the humor may be the only way through it. Take a recess! Remember when we were kids and we would go out and play and then come in and have cookies and milk? Remember how it was the best part of the school day?

As adults, we are so bogged down in responsibilities, goals, and "gotta dos" that we sometimes forget to enjoy ourselves. Well, guess what? You're in charge now. You get to pick the time for recess and when you get the cookies and milk. **What on earth are you waiting for? Do it today—don't wait!**

I have a reason for putting making the previous

sentences bold. Earlier in the book—Chapter 8, to be exact—I told the story of working the children's oncology ward at the Kansas University Medical Center.

One of the children I was performing for that day wanted a kazoo like the one I was using in my act. I told him I would bring him one in two days. Keep in mind, I only lived 10 minutes away from the medical center. When I called two days later to arrange the kazoo exchange, I found out the boy had died.

I'll never wait again. I will not put off doing the things I know will bring joy to myself and others. Who knows what will happen two days from now?

But no matter what happens, remember:

- Could be worse, could be raining.
- Live long, die short.
- If we're not laughing, we're puking or crying.
- Hope you get back on your foot.
- Superman don't need an airplane.
- Quit moving furniture in there.
- Smile, you're on candid camera.
- We're not midgets, it's just a costume.

I sincerely hope *You Just Have to Laugh* has allowed you to uncover your **jester**. I hope its shown you that laughter is the perfect **BOING** to stress. Never leave your house without some **humor grenades** and a **fun house mirror**, so you can laugh at yourself or whatever life throws you. The bottom line is when you laugh, you feel good. And isn't that the premise, babe?

Keep amused!
David Naster

You Just Have To Laugh
Comes to you

David Naster, who travels throughout the world making people laugh, would like to visit your corner of the world. His "You Just Have To Laugh" presentation shows us the value and power of humor and laughter.

You'll laugh, you'll smile; you might even shed a heartfelt tear, as David shares with you how fellow human beings have laughed their way through life's greatest challenges. He will also give you the tools to expand your **humorous perspective** in all facets of your life.

The true heart of David's presentation comes from the everyday things we all encounter and how we can appreciate their humorous angle.

David Naster speaks to *Fortune 500* companies, professional associations, government agencies (CIA included), religious groups, and small businesses, and he welcomes any group of humans who need a good laugh. (He is still working on other species.)

Contact David at:
888/815-8119 — Toll Free
913/438-4870 — Fax
naster@qni.com — E-mail
www.naster.com — Website

I need your help

Book two is now being compiled. If you have any true stories about how humor and laughing have helped you or someone you know get through a difficult or challenging time, please pass them on. Here are some of the categories I am looking for.

You Just Have To Laugh:

At relationships; spouses, friends, dating

At your relatives and family

At religion

At school

At your job

At the news

At politics

At sports

At just trying to survive each day

Please feel free to contact me at any of the following:

888/815-8119 — Toll Free

913/438-4870 — Fax

naster@qni.com — E-mail

www.naster.com — Website

Read these books
(you won't be sorry)

Hail to the Chiefs by Bob Gretz
Guide to Life by Sinbad
God said, Ha by Julia Sweeney
Anatomy of an Illness by Norman Cousins
The Mind Hunter by John Douglas
The Healing Power of Humor by Allen Klein
Voices from the Holocaust by Sylvia Rothchild
Harnessing Your Motivation by Denney Dey
Hitting the Highlights by Ernie Stautner
Laughter in Hell — Humor During the Holocaust
    by Steve Lipman
It's Not What Happens To You, It's What You Do
    About It by W. Mitchell
One Step At A Time by Bob Wieland
I'm No Hero and The Last Domino by Charlie
    Plumb

Attention motivational speakers
(in case you're tempted)

You know who you are. You are the ones who steal comedians' bits and make your living off of their creativity. I sincerely and firmly request that you honor the dignity of the people who have shared their stories in this book. When you lift any of these stories for your personal gain, please have the common courtesy to let your audience know these individuals' names and true stories. Taking "poetic license" means you are lying.